Praise for "Tragedy: Find

MW00658715

"I was deeply affected by the truths you found in simple tales. Your book has a wonderful message of hope as we all search for the meaning in suffering. Your book is excellently and poignantly written." *Adina Wrobleski, Author of Suicide: Why? and Suicide Survivors*

"I read the manuscript in one day because I could hardly put it down. It would not only be helpful to someone in the grieving process, but to anyone. Very meaningful!"
Carol Nord, Learning Disabilities Specialist

"Honest and insightful. I greatly admire the work you've done. I read most of it in one sitting. Very interesting."
Lu Harter, freelance proofreader

"Well-written and knowledgeable. I especially enjoyed the use of analogies between ourselves and characters found in Greek mythology. It was like reading a mirror of one's self. The segment on dreams is also highly relevant. An especially touching piece of work." *Mary Weaver, English Teacher*

"This book was captivating. It is sure to touch the hearts of anyone who is trying to find meaning behind any tragedy. Trudy's well-written and well-researched book is relevant for everyone. I especially appreciated her ability to find similarities between religions so as to narrow the gap between people and cultures. Timely in today's society."
Robin Blatnik, English and Composition Instructor

Tragedy:
Finding a Hidden Meaning

How to Transform the Tragedies in Your Life into Personal Growth

by
Trudy Carlson

First Edition

Benline Press
Duluth, Minnesota

ISBN 09642443-3-0
Library of Congress No. 95-94111

Benline Press, 118 N. 60th Avenue East
Duluth, Minnesota 55804

Publisher's Cataloging in Publication Data
Carlson, Trudy M.
Tragedy: Finding a Hidden Meaning How to Transform the Tragedies in Your Life Into Personal Growth
Includes bibliographical references and Index
1. Suffering.
2. Wisdom in Literature.
3. Spiritual formation.
4. Dreams.
5. Self-Actualization (Psychology).
BF789.S8 158/.1 95-94111
09642443-3-0

Table of Contents

Acknowledgment

No book is the product of just one person. My heartfelt gratitude goes to everyone who contributed to it. I want to thank those individuals who read this work in manuscript form at various stages. They include: Tracy Pierson, Marj Cox, Ann Sanford, Eileen Gannon, Carol Michealson, Roseann Biever, Lu Harter, Mary Weaver, Adina Wrobleski, Jo Stewart, Carol Nord, Rev. Edward Morgan, Monica Natzel, Caroline Carlson, Lena Biever, Garry Carlson, Char Gallian, Adela Hartman, Nancy Scheftner, Dr. Jerome Kwako, and Ben Wolfe.

I would like to make special mention of Kristen Oberg, Patt Jackson, and Robin Blatnik, the editors of the book, whose skill and encouragement helped to make it what it is. Their sustained commitment to this project is the kind of help writers dream of receiving, but never expect to get.

I wish to express appreciation to all the works that are quoted in this book. The list of these are contained in the bibliography.

There can be no full accounting of the debt I owe to the scores of people who contributed to this project by giving me advice and/or technical assistance. They include Joseph Gallian, James Perlman, and Sheldon Aubut.

The cover is designed by David Garon, and the painting on the cover is by Garry Carlson.

Chapter 1

Why I Wrote This Book

This book was written after the death of my only son, Ben. It is a result of my struggle to find an answer to what his life and his death meant both to him and me. Since childhood, I have been passionately questioning the meaning of life. I long to know what makes me the way I am, what makes other people think or act the way they do, and how life could be made better for all of us. In my search for answers to the mystery of life, I studied literature devoted to psychology and mythology. When Ben died, I used what I read to piece together a meaning for his illness and death.

At birth Ben looked like a normal baby, but the day I brought him home from the hospital, I was aware that he did not eat or sleep as well as his sister had when she was a newborn. Ben's problems with eating and sleeping persisted throughout infancy. There were other clues that all was not developing well; during preschool years he did not play well with other children and was unusually fearful. Although he interacted warmly with adults who helped him and allowed him to feel safe, he lacked social skills with peers. Ben was bright, but had trouble getting focused and staying focused on most tasks.

In first grade, his inability to concentrate and complete assignments indicated a learning problem. His father and I tried several times to obtain help for him from the school system but were unsuccessful. In sixth grade, Ben was evaluated at the Mayo Clinic in Rochester, Minnesota, where he was formally diagnosed as being depressed and having an attention deficit disorder. ADD is a condition characterized by an inability to pay attention and to be organized with tasks and assignments. Ben also suffered from frequent headaches, stomach aches, and pains in his arms and legs. Depression in children is frequently accompanied by physical pain as well as emotional pain. Since depression is a body illness, the physical pain is real and is often chronic.

Because he did not qualify for special services from the school system in our town, we arranged for private tutoring to help Ben deal with his learning problems. Though he resisted receiving psychiatric care immediately after the evaluations from the Mayo Clinic, he did start the low dosage of an antidepressant medication recommended by the team of physicians.

Depressive illness often is more prominent during adolescence when the biological changes characteristic of that stage in life combine with increased social pressures. School was becoming increasingly difficult for Ben with his limited ability to concentrate. His genetically-based depression was emerging steadily with each year. The two conditions (attention deficit and depression) meant Ben faced overwhelming demands. At the end of his first year in junior high this thirteen-year-old was seen by most of his teachers and peers as a typical kid. At home we knew he needed help. It would be some time before we would fully realize the effect a third condition, anxiety disorder and the panic attacks which often accompany it, had on Ben. We just know that all aspects of Ben's life were fraught with difficulty.

The summer prior to his eighth grade we got a better diagnosis of his depression. Ben had Bipolar II, a mood disorder characterized by alternating moods: high moods that do not get outrageously high, and lows that were very painful for him and made him irritable. After receiving the diagnosis of his particular type of depression and a referral to the child and adolescent psychiatry division of the University of Minnesota Hospitals in Minneapolis, Ben was willing to begin therapy and try new medications. He began by taking lithium. Later, the then new antidepressant, Prozac, was added. We were becoming optimistic about Ben's future. Unfortunately, during a trial reduction in his lithium, Ben, then fourteen, committed suicide.

Ben was not a perfect child, but his death occurred while he was complying with our attempts to get proper medical treatment for his condition. He was obeying his parents and following doctor's orders by taking his medications. He also complied with the reduction of lithium, a trial meant to discover if the medication was effective and necessary, or if it could be eliminated. His untimely death could be interpreted as just a mistake, or a meaningless tragedy. I refuse to see it that way.

This book is a very personal work. Most surviving family members ask, "Why did he or she commit suicide?" Research can tell us who is at risk for suicide; genetics experts can point to the inherited predisposition to certain depressive illnesses. Science can tell me **that** I had a child with a particular illness, but it cannot answer **why** this happened to him and to our family. When any of us anguish over "Why me?", one has to look to something other than science.

In his book, Courage to Create, psychologist Rollo May (1975) wrote that one does not write because one knows something. One writes to discover something. I wrote to discover a meaning for Ben's illness, and the value, and the benefits that could be gained from it. In order to do this, I turned to the stories our ancestors composed that address the mysteries of life. In these rich, enduring, yet seemingly simple stories lie the clues. Interpreting these stories is a way of deriving meaning from a seemingly meaningless tragedy. I would encourage anyone to use this method when confronting a painful life situation. The discoveries each of you make may not be of universal validity, but they will have profound personal meaning.

After finding a deeply satisfying answer to the meaning behind Ben's pain, I then went on to explore the issue of suffering and the value it has for personal growth. I found many insights from the experiences others had in overcoming difficulties. Concentration camp survivor, Dr. Victor Frankl, was especially helpful in my understanding of the way in which a painful life circumstance can provide personal development.

Finally, I sought to explore the role of fate. Are tragedies meant to happen? Are they part of some mysterious plan our lives are destined to follow? Or are they just bad luck? I have come to believe that life **does** follow a plan, and we can begin to understand destiny's course when we take seriously the clues provided by our own inner wisdom. Clues may come in the form of powerful dreams or through dramatic coincidences. Both of these are important sources of information regarding the direction our life is meant to take. Life is often painful, but what happens to us is seldom a mistake, seldom a meaningless accident.

Writing this book has brought me comfort and has taught me a great deal. It has allowed me to discover what may have been behind the suffering Ben experienced with his three problems: his anxiety disorder, depression, and attention deficit. It has allowed me to see everlasting value in his life for him and for me.

Presented here is an exploration of great stories. Some are tales that continue to live after hundreds or thousands of years. Others are stories from the lives of people who lived in the twentieth century. All of them focus on the purpose of life. I hope these tales will bring the same comfort to you that they brought to me. Though I lost my fourteen-year-old son, I realize that bereaved parents do not have a corner on suffering. Any painful loss -- the loss of one's job, the loss of a spouse through death or divorce, the loss of one's health, a loss resulting from an accident, the loss of a friend, the loss of money or one's home, or even a lost opportunity -- all produce suffering and grief. Perhaps this book can help you search for the meaning in suffering and find some answers when you ask, "Why me?"

Chapter 2

Suffering: The Task of Life

In the weeks and months following my son's death, I focused on the suffering he must have experienced during his life. In Grief and Bereavement in Contemporary Society, author Adina Wrobleski (1988) writes: "As might be expected for other causes of death in which great pain is experienced, 67% of the suicide survivors said they were relieved that the person was no longer suffering." There is no easy answer when confronted with the question of why a child should have to suffer. Thinking about Ben's troubled life, I felt a need to find some purpose for it, some benefit that would somehow make all his pain worthwhile. I wanted some ancient source of wisdom to prove his pain would be of some lasting good.

While I concentrated on his suffering, others in my family had a different perspective of Ben. I was gently reminded by one of my sisters that his life was not exclusively painful. At times it was filled with great joy. The side of Ben she saw was the smiling boy who enjoyed being around adults. Each of us focused on opposite sides of Ben's paradoxical nature. Thinking about these very different views of his life made me aware that a balanced perspective was needed. But where would I begin to find this balance?

The Wisdom found in Fairy Tales

For some time I have had a great respect for the wisdom found in fairy tales. Many people think of fairy tales as merely fanciful children's stories, unworthy of serious attention by mature adults. But for people interested in the psychological interpretation of stories, fairy tales are a treasury of ancient wisdom. When confronted with painful, seemingly senseless challenges, fairy tales can be of great help in dealing with the paradoxical and mysterious nature of life. Spending some time taking a close look at these enduring stories is a means of finding clues on how to cope with some of the most difficult problems in life.

One of the common themes found in fairy tales is that of a foolish boy who ends up marrying the princess and becoming the ruler of the kingdom. Often the story will start with an older man who has three sons. Two of the boys are smart and can easily manage all of life's demands. The parents show favoritism towards their clever sons. As the fairy tale progresses, some sort of trial presents itself, and each boy tries to meet the challenge. Much to everyone's amazement, it is the foolish son who succeeds.

After Ben's death, I read many books on depression, suicide, and grief. I did a lot of crying as I read them. I began to wonder if these books were really helpful or if they were only making me feel worse. They focused my attention exclusively on the issues surrounding Ben's pain and my loss. Although I was learning a lot of scientific information about Ben's condition, these books were not necessarily comforting.

What I needed was a balanced approach to my grief work. Consequently, I decided to read books not only on depression, but also great stories including fairy tales. I will always be grateful for books like The Good News about Depression, by Dr. Mark Gold, and Moodswings, by Dr. Ronald Fieve which I would read early in the evening. But right before I went to sleep each night, I would pick up Grimms' Tales For Young and Old. I opened the book at random, hoping the story I found would have significance to Ben's life.

The first two tales I read were both about boys described as blockheads. I wondered if there was some significance to this coincidence. The first one I read was "The Golden Goose." Reading it seriously, with the intent of applying it to my present situation and Ben's life, proved to be a very meaningful experience. Here is the first tale.

THE GOLDEN GOOSE

There was once a man who had three sons, and the youngest, who was called Blockhead, was despised, scoffed at and put down on every occasion. One day the eldest son decided to go into the forest and cut wood, and before he went his mother gave him a fine pancake and a bottle of wine to stave off his hunger and thirst. When he got to the forest, he met a little old gray man, who bade him good day and said: "I'm so hungry and thirsty. Give me a piece of that pancake you have in your pocket, and a drink of your wine." The clever son said: "If I give you my cake and wine, I won't have any for myself. Don't bother me." And left the little man standing there. He started to chop a tree down, and a moment later he missed his aim, his ax hit him in the arm, and he had to go home and get bandaged. That was the little gray man's doing.

Next the second son went into the forest, and his mother gave him a pancake and a bottle of wine, as she had the eldest. He too met the little old gray man, who asked him for a piece of his pancake and a drink of his wine. But the second son too replied cleverly: "What I give you I won't have for myself. Don't bother me." And left the little man standing there. He didn't have long to wait for his punishment. After the first few strokes at the tree he hit himself in the leg and had to be carried home.

Then Blockhead said: "Father, let me go out and cut wood." His father replied: "Your brothers have tried it and hurt themselves, you'd better leave it alone, you don't know the first thing about wood cutting." But Blockhead begged and pleaded until finally the father said: "All right, go ahead, if you get hurt it will teach you to know better." His mother gave him a pancake made of water and ashes and a bottle of sour beer. When he got to the forest, he too met the little old gray man, who greeted him and said: "I'm so hungry and thirsty. Give me a piece of your pancake and a drink out of your bottle." Blockhead replied: "All I've got is an ash cake and some sour beer: if that suits you, come sit down and have some." They sat down, and when Blockhead brought out his ash cake, it was a fine pancake and the sour beer was good wine. They ate and drank, and when they had finished the little man said: "Because you have a good heart and cheerfully share what's yours, I'll give you good luck. See that old tree over there? Cut it down and you'll find something in the roots." Then the little man left him.

Blockhead cut the tree down, and when it fell there was a goose in the roots with feathers of pure gold. He picked the goose up in his arms and went to an inn for the night. The innkeeper had three daughters, and when they saw the goose they were curious to know more about the strange bird. They all coveted the golden feathers, and the eldest thought: "I'll surely get a chance to pluck one of them." When Blockhead went off to bed, she grabbed the goose's wing, but her finger and hand stuck fast. A little later the second came along, and her only thought was to pluck a golden feather. But no sooner had she touched her sister then she stuck fast. Finally, the third came in with the same purpose. The two others cried out: "Keep away, for heaven's sake, keep away!" But she didn't see why she should keep away. "Why shouldn't I go where they are?" she thought, and ran over to them, touched her sister and stuck fast. So they all had to spend the night with the goose.

Next morning Blockhead picked the goose up in his arms and started off. He paid no attention to the three girls who were hanging on to it, and they had to keep running after him, now left, now right, whichever way he happened to go. As they were trotting down a country lane, the parson came along. When he saw the procession he said: "Horrid girls, you ought to be ashamed! Why are you chasing this young fellow? Do you think it's nice?" With that he grabbed the youngest by the hand and tried to pull her back, but the moment he touched her, he too stuck fast and had to run along with the others. In a little while the sexton came by. When he saw the pastor running after the three girls, he cried out in amazement: "Hey, Reverend, where are you going so fast? Don't forget, we've got a christening today." He ran after him, took him by the sleeve, and stuck fast. As the five of them trotted along, they passed two peasants coming from the fields with their hoes. The parson called to the peasants for help, but no sooner had they touched the sexton than they stuck fast, and now there were seven running after Blockhead and his goose.

Later in the day he came to a city where there was a king whose daughter was so solemn that no one could make her laugh. He had decreed that the first man to make her laugh should have her for his wife. When Blockhead heard that, he went before the king's daughter with his goose and its retinue, and when she saw the seven of them running along in a chain, she burst out laughing, and it looked as if she'd never stop. So Blockhead claimed her as his wife, but the king didn't approve of him as a son-in-law and raised all sorts of objections. Finally he said that before Blockhead could marry his daughter he'd have to bring him a man who could drink up a whole cellar full of wine. Blockhead thought the little gray man might help him and went out into the forest. In the place where he had chopped the tree down he saw a very unhappy-looking man sitting on the ground. Blockhead asked him what the trouble was, and the man replied: "I've got such a thirst that I can't quench it. Cold water doesn't agree with me. I've just drunk up a whole barrel of wine, but that's only a drop in the bucket." "I can help you," said Blockhead. "Come with me and you'll get your fill." Thereupon he led him to the king's cellar, and the man set to work on the great hogsheads. He drank and drank till his sides ached, and before the day was out he had drained the whole cellar. Again Blockhead claimed his bride, but the king was so reluctant to let this dolt, whom everybody called Blockhead, marry his daughter, that he thought up a new condition: now he wanted a man who could eat a whole mountain of bread. Blockhead didn't have to think very long. He went out into the forest, and in the very same place found a man who was tightening a belt around his belly and making the most miserable face. "I've eaten a whole ovenful of bread," the man said, "but with a hunger like mine that's as good as nothing. My belly is as empty as ever and if I didn't strap it tight my hunger would kill me." Blockhead was glad to hear it. "Come with me," he said, "and you'll eat your fill." He took him to the courtyard of the king's palace. All the flour in the whole kingdom had been brought there and baked into a huge mountain of bread. But the man from the forest stepped right up and began to eat, and in a single day the whole mountain was gone.

Blockhead claimed his bride for the third time, but the king thought up still another condition. Now he wanted a ship that could sail both on land and on water. "But as soon as you bring me that ship you shall have my daughter," he said. Blockhead went straight into the forest, and there sat the little gray man he had given his pancake to. "I've drunk and I've eaten for you," he said, "and I'll give you your ship too. I'm doing all this because you were kind to me." So he gave him the ship that sailed both on land and on water. When the king saw it, he couldn't deny him his daughter any longer, and the marriage was celebrated. At the king's death

Blockhead inherited the kingdom and lived happily with his wife for many years. (Manheim, 1977, pp. 242-245)

This seemingly simple yet complex fairy tale, like all great stories, can be explained in many different ways because it lends itself to both personal and general meaning. I interpreted this story with special application to my son; someone who did not appear to succeed in life, and who suffered much pain. By showing how this story can be paraphrased to provide personal meaning, I will demonstrate how anyone can use this method when confronted with a tragedy. To unlock the meaning of the tale, it is necessary to go step by step taking it apart.

Application of the Wisdom within the tale

At the very beginning of this tale we learn that Blockhead was despised, scoffed at, and put down on every occasion. I wonder if that is not the way a child with a learning disability and depression experiences life? His perception of being rejected and ridiculed comes from two separate sources. First, many of these children have an overly sensitive nature. The usual comments adults and peers make to them often are interpreted by them as insults. They feel others are being critical of them, when this may not be the case at all. Secondly, since these children do actually have difficulty with school work, with following the rules of games, and with figuring out how to interact with peers, there is in fact some basis for their feelings of being despised, scoffed at and put down on every occasion.

The parents in this story favored the two older boys. Children who can handle life's demands are easier for parents to deal with than youngsters who can not. Although parents are often sympathetic towards children who are having difficulty with their lives, it is also true that these children's problems make the parents' lives difficult, too. There is a tendency for parents to appreciate and feel grateful for children who are easy to raise, simply because it makes their own lives less stressful.

On the other hand, when reading "The Golden Goose," our compassion for Blockhead's plight may cause us to be judgmental towards the parents for their favoritism towards the clever sons. Perhaps our compassion can be expanded to include the entire family. The parents are, after all, only reacting as the whole culture reacts. Whether it is at school, at work, or in a social situation, life is just easier when people can do what is expected of them and get along with one another. Society favors people who are capable. Often we come to see them as "good" and "deserving," whereas people with less ability are seem as "bad" and "undeserving." The older sons in this tale are given wine and a fine pancake. Blockhead is given a pancake made of ashes and water along with a bottle of sour beer. He is given things that might normally be thrown away, things appropriate for someone who does not deserve better.

Now comes the first of a series of trials in the fairy tale. The eldest son goes into the forest to chop wood. He meets an old gray man who asks him to share what he has. The clever son gives the old man an economically realistic response, "If I give you my cake and wine, I won't have any for myself. Don't bother me." What does this mean? The son leaves the established society (his family) and enters the forest. This can symbolize a turning from the world of other people's demands and expectations, to turning towards the inner psyche, the place where clues to one's personal destiny are available. This search for personal inner guidance to discover one's fate is the function of the Native American's vision quest. The clever son encounters an inner wisdom figure. It asks the boy to give something of himself to inner life. Reluctant to do so, the clever son makes it clear he does not want to be bothered with the spiritual aspects of life. When the clever son rejects the call of his inner spiritual nature, his refusal affects him. When he denies the legitimate demands of his inner life by stubbornly focusing only on the outer world, the force within makes him stop. The boy has an accident with an ax, cutting his arm, and he goes back home.

The story continues with the typical pattern found in many fairy tales. The second son, who is also clever, goes out to chop wood and has exactly the same experience as his older brother. This repetition serves to point out that most people think and act like the clever sons. Most of us concern ourselves with outer practical matters. It is only the unusual person who pays attention to inner life. The typical pattern in fairy tales echoes the typical pattern all of us follow in the course of our lives. It is only after we have been injured a number of times that we are finally willing to respond to the call of the inner spirit. It takes a number of painful accidents for us to give part of ourselves to inner demands.

After the two clever sons hurt themselves, it is Blockhead's turn to try cutting wood. His father does not trust his blockhead son to succeed when his other more capable sons have failed. His father has not seen any evidence that Blockhead could do anything right; there is no reason to expect Blockhead would be able to do so now. The father ridicules Blockhead's request, but after a while he does allow him to go. This part of the story has special resonance for me. When my son entered junior high he wanted to join the band. Ben had so much trouble learning anything that I had a hard time imagining he could tackle a musical instrument. Like Blockhead in the story, my son had a hard time convincing me that I should let him try.

Blockhead sets out for the woods carrying with him some sour beer and ash pancake his mother gave to him. When he meets the old gray man, he is willing to share, to give of himself. Perhaps it is precisely his lack of outer success that makes him more open to the plight of others. Perhaps his past experience with ridicule made him more sensitive to rejection and less willing to reject the requests of others. Like Blockhead, depressed people are often sensitive to the pain of others because they know how it feels.

When Blockhead brings out the pancake made of ashes and water, it is transformed into a fine pancake. His sour beer becomes good wine. In the spiritual domain, "despised, scoffed at and put down" experiences are turned into something positive. The symbols of rejection, the ash pancake and sour beer, are transformed. The things which are most painful are the very things capable of "nourishing" the inner spirit of the person.

Blockhead does not tell the old man, "don't bother me" as his clever brothers had done. It is his willingness to pay attention to the old man and to honor his request that transforms the boy's outer circumstance. Blockhead is willing to listen to the old man who tells him to cut down a special tree. There he will find at its root a goose "with feathers of pure gold." At the root of the tree, Blockhead finds a golden goose.

Gold is an important element in fairy tales. In Interpretation of Fairy Tales, Marie Louis von Franz (1970) describes the meaning of gold:

> Gold is everlasting and in former times was the only known metal which did not decay or become black or green and resisted all corrosive elements. Gold treasures can be buried in the earth and dug up unharmed after a thousand years, as is not the case with copper or silver or iron, so it is the immortal, the transcendental element, that which outlasts ephemeral existence; it is the eternal, the divine and the most precious, and whenever something is made of gold it is said to have that eternal quality.

When an object in a fairy tale is made of gold, it denotes something of great and everlasting value. Blockhead finds the goose at the root of the special tree, the source of its life. This object denotes that at the source of the tree of life is an incorruptible, divine element.

The golden object in this story is in the form of a goose. In Shadow and Evil in Fairy Tales, von Franz (1987) describes the goose as a paradoxical symbol. Geese are stupid; we have all heard the term, "a silly goose." But von Franz reminds us that in ancient Greece, the goose...

> “represented a special aspect of Mother Nature or the nature Goddess, Nemesis. Nemesis comes from the word *nemo* , which means to distribute, to attribute to each one his right lot. Nemesis is a principle of natural justice by which everyone gets what they deserve. We cannot avoid seeing that there is such a principle in the unconscious which has a curious way of giving to people exactly what one feels is somehow deserved. It is not justice in the human sense of the word, but there is an uncanny regulating force in nature which acts like justice and strikes one as being meaningful.”

I find the symbol of the goose comforting when I interpret it in light of my son's life. With his attention deficit, his anxiety, and his depression, Ben in many ways acted like the Blockhead in this story. It is heartening to see that silly, stupid Blockhead gets what he truly deserves, something that counter-balances the painful experiences he had during his lifetime. Personally interpreted, this fairy tale implies that what Ben will ultimately receive is what he in fact deserves. He receives this gift as a result of his willingness to recognize and contribute to his inner life. The goose is a seemingly silly object that provides its own type of justice. It has great value, the complete worth of which is only appreciated as the story unfolds.

Blockhead now goes to an inn. The innkeeper's three daughters are curious to know more about the strange bird.

These girls who have no gifts of the spirit from their own life experiences choose to try taking some of what Blockhead has. Of course it does not work. The eldest is the first to get stuck trying to steal a feather; the same happens to the second daughter. The two older girls try to warn their youngest sister against doing what they did. But young people seldom listen or learn from the mistakes of others. They often need to learn things for themselves. The youngest daughter goes through the same process as her sisters and gets stuck just as they did.

The next morning Blockhead pays no attention to his new following and continues on his path. A parson tries to stop the girls from being carried away with Blockhead, but he too ends up becoming one of the followers. This is an interesting point. Blockhead had his own spiritual experience. The parson, although a scholar of religious ideas, becomes a follower of the man with a personal experience of the spirit. Blockhead acquires quite an entourage. A sexton joins him, as do some peasants. The golden goose, which came as a result of an experience with the spiritual domain, has the power to carry people along a path even against their conscious intentions.

Blockhead and his group come to a city. The king of the realm has a problem: there is something wrong with his daughter. The king had decreed that whoever healed her could have her as his bride. Blockhead's silly goose and its seven followers make her laugh. This part of the fairy tale points out the connection between laughter and healing. Eastern monks and Native Americans have long honored the connection. Western tradition, in the past, has not always emphasized it. Today the medical profession is recognizing the importance of humor in healing.

In the fairy tale, the king objects to Blockhead as a son-in-law. Though the father is worried by his daughter's solemn nature, he is reluctant to accept the cure when it involves a Blockhead. To prevent the marriage, the king sets up further tests. In fairy tales, as in life, there are a number of difficult trials in any venture. The additional tests would be impossible if Blockhead attempts to complete them with ordinary means. They are only possible when Blockhead goes back to the inner domain (the forest) and seeks out the help of the spirit within.

I think of my son in terms of the Blockhead symbol. Although Ben was incapable of succeeding in the outer world, his life was a success in the inner domain. He was a mature, perceptive young man of wisdom and depth. Like Blockhead in this story, the pain Ben experienced in this life is exactly what can be used to develop the spiritual dimension. Ben did not fit in well. The rejected Blockhead in this story reminds me of a quote I have often heard in church: "The stone which the builders rejected has become the cornerstone." (Psalm 118: 22) When constructing a building, it is easier when all the stones are the same size (i.e. when people fit into a system). The oddball shape does not fit in, and is consequently rejected. But perhaps it is precisely the rejected stone that is the cornerstone in a different system -- the spiritual domain. The painful trials one experiences are opportunities for personal growth.

I hope I will not be misunderstood. I do not mean to imply we should deliberately court misfortune and rejection. We should not try to make life difficult for ourselves or others. We need to make an effort to make our lives work. But if one is confronted with what appears to be an impossible situation, rather than become bitter about misfortune, we can feel consoled with the knowledge that it is the spiritual domain which is being served. It is in the spiritual realm we will get our "just desserts." This theory is not meant to encourage a premature entrance into the afterlife. Rather, it can help decrease needless suffering by giving meaning to the pain we experience during our lifetime. Suffering is of lasting value when seen as a means of developing depth for the personality and growth of the spirit within.

The role of suffering is difficult to discern. Victor Frankl, a Viennese survivor of World War II concentration camps, maintains that one can accept suffering as bearable because suffering is the source of growth. I, too, wish to honor the necessary suffering in life, while cautioning against unnecessary suffering. Necessary, unavoidable suffering can produce spiritual growth, but paradoxically, we also have an obligation to do the best we can to live our lives in a positive manner which avoids difficulties of our own making. It is sometimes hard to know the difference between our "God given" suffering, which adds depth to life, and the trouble we cause ourselves and others when we create unnecessary problems. I think one of the best expressions of this dilemma is contained in the Serenity Prayer. "God grant me the serenity to accept the things I cannot change, the courage to change the things I can, and the wisdom to know the difference."

Keeping in mind that suffering is the coin that buys spiritual growth, and at the same time trying to avoid unnecessary suffering, thoughtful persons who wish to develop their spirituality may ask, "Is there any constructive way to grow spiritually at times in life when things are going well?" I remember asking myself a similar question when I was a child. I recall hearing in church, "Amen, I say to you, it will be hard for one who is rich to enter the kingdom of heaven. Again I say to you, it is easier for a camel to pass through the eye of a needle than for one who is rich to enter the kingdom of God." (Matthew 19: 23-24) If that were literally true, then the only people who would be going to heaven would be poor people! That did not make any sense to me. I knew many good people with wealth and some not so good people who were poor. It did not seem that money was necessarily correlated with virtue.

Another time in church I recall hearing, "But woe to you who are rich, for you have received your consolation. But woe to you who are filled now, for you will be hungry. Woe to you who laugh now, for you will grieve and weep. Woe to you when all speak well of you, for their ancestors treated the false prophets in this way." (Luke 6: 24-26)

When taken literally, these verses would also imply that you should never rejoice in your good fortune; that one should actually invite misfortune and suffering. There are several valid interpretations to the idea that fortunate people have difficulty getting into the kingdom. One of them is that persons who are not given a lot of difficult trial in their lifetime may not grow spiritually unless they consciously choose to be compassionate to others who are suffering. In choosing compassion, one actively seeks to share another person's suffering. The compassionate are in tune with the suffering of others, and act to relieve pain.

By relieving suffering you are not actually taking their pain away from them. No one is capable of fixing another person's problems and eliminating discomfort. Being compassionate often consists of carefully listening to someone else tell you their story. In allowing someone else to cry, to express anger, disappointment, and sorrow, one shares in their pain and for a time helps to reduce it. Pain is often referred to as a heavy weight that an individual is carrying. During the time one is carefully listening and putting oneself in tune with another's pain, the burden is lessened. It is analogous to two people carrying a heavy box rather than one person trying to carry it alone.

I interpreted "The Golden Goose" as the tale of a person who was unsuccessful at meeting the demands and expectations of life but was willing to pay attention to the inner guidance. He receives justice (the golden goose) and his future trials (otherwise insurmountably difficult tests) are successfully handled when he relies on this inner wisdom.

Cynics may see this as just the old "more-pie-in-the-sky-bye-and-bye." On one level it may be just that. But this story helped me feel my son's suffering was not simply unnecessary pain. Although he lacked success when judged by one set of criteria, he developed spiritually by paying attention to his own inner wisdom. His sensitivity, and his willingness to pay attention to sources of inner guidance, was like that of the Blockhead in the tale. It serves to lend credence to applying this particular story and its outcome to Ben's life.

It is my belief that fairy tales are meant for us to interpret on a personal level as well as on universal terms.

Chapter 3

Trusting Fate

When I was a child, I wondered why the lazy boy always ends up doing exactly the right thing in fairy tales. It is the foolish son who always wins the princess, while the clever sons end up losers. I asked myself, "Does this mean I am wasting my time working hard studying in school? Does success in life really turn out to be a matter of dumb luck?"

These questions speak to a second aspect of the Blockhead symbol. The Blockhead puts himself in tune both with the force of nature within himself and with the will of God. By putting himself in tune with these powerful forces, he is able to effortlessly do just exactly the right thing. He is aligned with forces much more profound than merely his personal intentions. This is probably what is meant in the Lord's Prayer: "Thy kingdom come, Thy will be done" -- not just my own agenda but the one I was **meant** to fulfill. Blockhead does not make decisions based solely with his intellect; he listens to his heart. Instead of frantically doing things he has decided to do, Blockhead relaxes into what presents itself next in life. Rather than fighting against what presents itself, Blockhead honors it.

This second aspect of the Blockhead symbol is exemplified by the second story I found as I randomly opened the fairy tale book.

The Three Feathers

There was once a King who had three sons. Two were clever, but the third was called Blockhead because he was simple and hardly opened his mouth. When the king became old and feeble and thought his end was near, he didn't know which of his sons to leave his kingdom to. So he called them together and said: "Go out and search, and the one who brings me the finest carpet shall be king after my death." And to make sure there would be no quarrel among them, he led them to a place outside the castle, blew three feathers into the air, and said: "Go as they fly." One feather flew east and another west, while the third flew straight ahead but not far, and soon fell to the ground. The first brother went right, the second brother went left, and they scoffed at Blockhead who had to stop where the third feather had fallen.

Blockhead sat down. He was very sad. Suddenly he caught sight of a trap door not far from the feather. He lifted it up, found a stairway, and went down. At the bottom there was another door. He knocked, and heard someone inside calling:

"Little green maid
Perched on a log,
Hobgoblin's dog,
Wobblin' goblin,
Quick, go and see,
What that knocking can be."

The door opened and there sat a big fat toad, surrounded by a crowd of little toads. The fat toad asked him what he wanted, and he replied: "I'm looking for the finest and most beautiful carpet in all the world." Whereupon she called one of the young toads and said:

"Little green maid
Perched on a log,
Hobgoblin's dog,
Wobblin's goblin,
That box you see,
Bring it here to me."

The young toad brought the box, the fat toad opened it, took out a carpet so fine that nothing like it could have been woven on the earth above, and gave it to Blockhead. He thanked her and went back up the stairs.

The two elder brothers had thought the youngest was much too stupid to find anything, much less bring it back. "Why," they said, "should we go to the trouble of searching?" So they stopped the first shepherdess they met, took the crude shawl she had on, and brought it back to the king. Blockhead had just arrived with his beautiful carpet. The king was amazed when he saw it and said: "By right the kingdom should go to the youngest." But the two others gave their father no peace. They said it just wouldn't do for Blockhead, who was a fool in every respect, to be king, and begged their father to set another task. At length he said: "The one who brings me the most beautiful ring shall inherit the kingdom." Again he took them outside, blew three feathers into the air, and bade them follow the feathers. Again the two eldest went east and west. Blockhead's feather flew straight ahead and fell near the trap door. Again he went down to the fat toad, and this time he told her he needed the most beautiful ring on the earth. She called for their big box, took out a ring which was set with glittering gems and was so beautiful that no goldsmith on earth could have made it, and gave it to Blockhead. The two elder brothers laughed at the thought of Blockhead looking for a golden ring. They went to no trouble at all but just hammered the nails out of the rim of an old cartwheel and brought it to the king. When Blockhead produced his gold ring, his father said: "The kingdom goes to him." But the two elder brothers kept nagging at their father until he set a third task. The kingdom, he said, would go to the one who brought back the most beautiful maid. Again he blew the three feathers into the air and again they flew as they had before.

Blockhead went straight to the fat toad and said: "I need the most beautiful maid in the world." "Well, well!" said the toad. "The most beautiful maid in the world isn't here right now, but you shall have her all the same." Whereupon she gave him a hollowed-out carrot with six mice harnessed to it. Blockhead asked her sadly: "What good will this do me?" The toad replied: "Just take one of my little toads and put her inside." He picked one out at random and put her into the carriage, and no sooner was she in it than she turned into a beautiful maiden, the carrot turned into a carriage, and the six mice turned into horses. Whereupon he kissed her, lashed the horses into a gallop, and brought her to the king. His brothers turned up a little later. They hadn't bothered to look for a beautiful maid, but they had taken the first peasant wenches they came across. When the king saw them, he said: "The kingdom will go to the youngest after my death." But again the two eldest fussed and fumed. "We can't let Blockhead be king!" they cried, and insisted that the brother whose wife could jump through a ring that was hanging in the middle of the hall should be chosen. They thought: "These peasant women are strong enough to do it; the sensitive damsel will only kill herself if she tries." Again the old king consented. When the two peasant women jumped, they managed to get through the ring, but they were so clumsy they fell and broke their big, thick arms and legs. Then the fair lady Blockhead had brought home jumped, and she glided through the ring as lightly and easily as a deer. After that there was nothing the brothers could say. The crown went to Blockhead, and he reigned wisely for many years. (Manheim, 1977, pp. 239-241)

Application of the Wisdom Within the Tale

Here is a story of no ordinary father, but a king. He acts with more wisdom than many fathers. Unlike the father in "The Golden Goose" who had a preconceived notion of which sons could succeed and showed favoritism towards his clever sons, the king in this story makes no judgments. When his reign comes to an end, the king does not put his trust in his own desires or wishes. He realizes something beyond his human perspective should determine who will be the next ruler of the kingdom. He sets up a competition and is willing to allow fate to determine the outcome. The son who proves himself worthy of the task will become the new king.

The story says the three sons are taken to a place outside the castle and they are to go in the direction their feather takes them. The king did not decide the direction or path his sons are to take. It is a wise father who does not interfere with the natural path his son is to follow. The king is aligning the fate of his kingdom with the will of a higher power. It is a force outside of anyone's conscious intention -- the winds of destiny. The sons are to follow the particular course of their own individual fate.

The lyrics of the old song, "Back in Your Own Backyard" says that after going to the east and to the west, some day, a little weary (perhaps a little older and wiser) you will come back to where your happiness was to be found all along -- right in your own backyard. Those lyrics summarize the direction Blockhead's feather pointed. The most direct route to the goal in life is right where you are.

The two clever brothers followed their feather. It took them far away, out into the world, the route they thought had greater potential for success in the contest of winning the kingdom. They scoffed at Blockhead, whose feather directed him not to go outwards and away, but to stop. The way to spiritual growth does not require a faraway journey, but an inward journey.

Blockhead is originally sad. It is precisely in his sadness, in his stillness, and in his pain, that the task is achieved. A famous quote of Meister Eckhardt is relevant here. I have heard two versions. The first is, "Suffering is the swiftest horse that brings you to perfection." The second is, "Suffering is the swiftest steed that brings you to wholeness." Both are wonderful ways of saying the fastest means towards personal growth are the tragedies of life. Eckhardt's words also say that the necessary suffering in life is not only unavoidable, but can be embraced.

Blockhead's feather fell to the earth. The earth is a rich symbol offering more than one interpretation. Blockhead's going down into the earth is a descent to the feminine, into Mother Earth. This is especially important in this particular fairy tale because what is missing at the beginning of the story is the feminine. There is a king and three sons; the queen is absent. When Blockhead goes into the earth he encounters a large toad surrounded by little toads. Why toads? "The toad has always been associated with the earth-mother." (von Franz, 1987, p. 53). As Blockhead goes down into the earth, he encounters what is necessary to bring wholeness to any successful future reign of the kingdom: femininity. This balance is exactly what is needed to help him to be a wise ruler. Perhaps this is why it was so important for the old king to trust a larger perspective and not rely on limited human thinking when determining who should be trusted with the future of the realm.

How does Blockhead treat these toads? First of all, he knocked before entering their chamber. By knocking, he shows the proper respect for this place and the power within Mother Earth. His task is to seek the objects his father commands him to find. The toad asks him what he wants.

Without any type of deception, manipulation, or cunning, he simply and respectfully asks the feminine power in the earth for what he needs. This kind of straightforward asking for what you need is encouraged in the Bible, "Ask and you shall receive, seek and you shall find, knock and it shall be opened unto you." The feminine power has the ability to grant his wish, and she gives him the finest carpet in the world. She gives it to him without expecting anything in return.

In life there is usually some price to pay for whatever is received. But in these tales, dealing with the mysteries of life, the solutions to extremely difficult tests are always freely supplied by the god or goddess who present themselves either as a helpful animal or curious stranger. Blockhead takes the rug from the toad and gives her his thanks. What is noteworthy is that he shows proper respect.

Compare Blockhead's approach to what the clever brothers did and what they failed to do. Instead of doing the task they were given in life, which was to go out and search and bring back the finest carpet, they made their own decision about what they would do. In other words, instead of performing their true mission, they made a decision based on their own personal desires. Their attitude was, "Why should I go through a lot of effort on an extensive search for something of value? I will do the easy thing; I'll grab the first thing I see."

They robbed a shepherdess of her crude shawl. Their theft is contrary to the respectful manner which Blockhead showed to the feminine. In response to the king's order to bring back a fine carpet, the clever sons offer him something that is not even a rug. They bring back a shawl. Their actions make it clear they are "off the mark," which is the ancient definition of the word **sin**. Sin may be doing what you desire when it contradicts the true purpose of your life.

There are four trials in this tale. Each of these four trials may be symbolic of the tasks each of us face during various stages of our lives. If life consists of four stages, i.e. childhood, youth, middle life and old age; and if it is true, as developmental psychologists have claimed, that each stage has a specific developmental task, then the trials in this fairy tale can be interpreted as symbolic of the four developmental tasks. Those who perform the task for the stage achieve the authentic purpose of their lives.

The goal for the first stage of life (childhood, ages 0-15) is the carpet. A carpet is something to stand on in life. Von Franz (1987b, pp. 55-56) writes,

> "The nomadic Arab tribes, who are still famous for their carpet weaving, say that the carpets they use in their tents represent that continuity of earth which they need to prevent them from feeling that they have no soil under their feet. Wherever they go they first spread one of those beautiful carpets on which they stand, as we do on our earth...the (carpet) designs are often used as a symbol for the complex symbolic patterns of life and the secret designs of fate. It represents the greater pattern of our life, which we do not know as long as we live it...so the carpet represents not only Mother Earth for those people but also the inner basis of their whole life."

Blockhead's possession of the carpet he received from his inward journey into Mother Earth gives him a basis for the pattern of his life which develops throughout the tale.

Blockhead completes the test and brings back the carpet. The king is willing to give the kingdom to Blockhead, but in fairy tales, as in life, there is a series of trials rather than just one. Although life's trials may seem different and unrelated to each other, they often have a common theme that only becomes clear as time goes on. When all of the jigsaw pieces of our life come together in old age, the final picture becomes clear. Or, as Von Franz says, sometimes the pattern in the carpet is only visible from a certain objective distance.

The second trial is to bring back the most beautiful ring. The task for the second stage of life (youth, ages 15-35) is the golden ring. Gold represents the eternal, and a ring is round with no beginning and no end. Von Franz (1970) says that as a circular object, the ring is a symbol used in many cultures to represent the central regulating factor of the psyche. Its function is to produce balance in a personality.

The story says the king again blows the three feathers to start the trial. Each son is given another chance to follow his true course in life. Real life also presents us with several opportunities to get on our intended path. The clever brothers are not wrong by following an outer path. The outward adventure is the destiny of those clever sons, just as it is Blockhead's fate to have an inward experience. The clever sons could have really gone on an adventure, going from kingdom to kingdom, searching high and low, first for the most beautiful carpet, now for the most beautiful ring. They did not have to take the first thing they saw. If they would have searched until they finally satisfied their hearts' goal and accomplished what their father asked of them, they would have respected their fate (the outward life) and gained the respect of the king. In many stories, the hero has the outer adventure. But these sons reject the true task of their lives. They refuse their call. They allow their conscious thinking to go against their fate. Their decision has nothing to do with what they really know is right. They only use their heads, instead of including their hearts. Off the mark again, they sin.

By contrast, Blockhead follows the direction his feather leads him. Again he is led inward. He tells the toad what he needs, and he receives it. This implies that there are vast resources within us if we ask. The clever sons who laugh when Blockhead's feather hits the ground reject the possibility that the inward path can produce anything of value. Blockhead's inward path gives him what he needs and what his father asked for.

At this point in the tale, Blockhead has already accomplished the childhood task of obtaining an original standpoint (a fundamental point of view) when he acquired the carpet. Now in youth, his development is deepened and enriched as he achieves connection to his self-regulating, balancing principle, symbolized by the golden ring.

Now he faces the third task in life, to bring back the most beautiful maid. This part of the tale is reminiscent of the story of Cinderella: six mice are turned into horses, an old carrot is turned into a carriage. When the toad first gives him the six mice and the carrot, Blockhead momentarily feels sad and does not show confidence in her. Nonetheless he follows her advice. When she tells him to pick one of her little toads, he puts a small toad inside the hollowed out carrot, whereby the toad is transformed into a beautiful maid. The process he used to pick out one of the toads is important. Instead of cleverly deciding what is best, he picked one out at random, trusting something other than his own personal opinion about what is good or bad, right or wrong.

This third goal, the task in mid-life, (ages 35-60's) was for the sons to get the most beautiful maiden. The maiden is a symbol for the inner feminine. The task involves joining the feminine characteristics with the masculine to produce wholeness in the personality. The marriage of the masculine and the feminine within an individual is appropriate as the task of mid-life, because it takes maturity in order to achieve it. I believe this is why marriage comes towards the end of most fairy tales we read.

The clever brothers hadn't bothered to look for a beautiful maiden, but had taken the first peasant wenches they came across. The crudeness with which the clever sons have acted in the past is matched by the crudeness of their peasant wenches. It is as if their wives are reflective of something within themselves -- their own inner feminine. They have never shown any respect for the feminine, and thus lack inner beauty. Blockhead, on the other hand, shows appreciation for the feminine, and the beautiful inner maiden is his reward. The king pronounces Blockhead the winner, the one who will rule after his death.

The clever sons give one final protest. Having failed at each of the trials which the king set up for them, the elder sons hope that by naming the task themselves they can cleverly manipulate the last trial to enable them to win. By choosing the ring-jumping contest, they hope the strength of their peasant wives will be an asset. They assume the sensitive damsel Blockhead married will not be fit for the task. But how can anyone outsmart destiny? Blockhead's maiden wins the competition, and this time he is finally made King.

The fourth and final task of life, accomplished in old age, is symbolized by the maiden going through the golden ring. In old age, health is something all of us want, but brute strength does not turn out to be important. The delicate maid which Blockhead won by following the correct attitude during mid-life is "right on the mark," and she goes through the ring "as lightly and easily as a deer."

Von Franz (1970, p. 66) points out that jumping through a ring requires that one jumps high, and at the same time aims "accurately at the center of the ring to get through it." This motif of aiming at or through the center of the ring is used by the Zen Buddhist when performing the art of archery. It is done as a "form of deep meditation by which the archer puts himself inwardly into his own center, from whence, naturally, he can hit the outer target." The whole practice is meant as a technique to help the person find the way to dwell in one's own inner center without being diverted by thought, ambition, or ego-impulse.

This is an appropriate task for the last years of life. During one's final years, wisdom and quiet peace can preside in the personality if the individual no longer is diverted by personal ambitions and impulses. Connected or directed by wholeness, people can begin to dwell more exclusively in their own inner center and let go of outer concerns. Doing this naturally allows them to hit the target.

What does this interpretation have to do with my grief for Ben? How is the Blockhead in this story like my son? Can "The Three Feathers" bring meaning to the suffering he went through in the same way that "The Golden Goose" did? The answer to this is found in the chapter that lies ahead. There you will find a more personal analysis of this story, similar to the kind of interpretation you too can choose to make of your own suffering.

Chapter 4

Putting the Horse Before the Cart

Each of the stories I encountered when randomly opening my fairly tales book taught me something different. The Golden Goose speaks of the value of the painful experiences of life and the importance of compassion. Those who suffer can have an everlasting, eternal reward that is a balance to the pain they experience. This occurs if they are willing to use their suffering for spiritual purposes and if they trust the meaning of life. People who find themselves in more fortunate circumstances are encouraged by this story to use opportunities to relieve the pain of others as a means for their own spiritual growth.

The Three Feathers taught me that spiritually developed people put themselves in tune with both the forces of nature within themselves (their fundamental biological/human nature) and with the will of God. By doing so, they lead an authentic life and fulfill developmental tasks to achieve a balance and wholeness throughout life.

Although the emphasis of the two fairy tales is different, the similarity is striking. There are three brothers, and four tasks. The seemingly impossible tasks are accomplished by a power outside of the rational world. In both stories, the Blockhead is scoffed at, ridiculed, and suffers.

Applying the wisdom of the tales to a personal tragedy

When I apply the lessons of these two stories to my son's life, I realize that neither Ben nor I were in charge of his life. I wanted a clever son - one who could do well in school, get along with other children, find joy in his family, have meaningful work as an adult, give me grandchildren and comfort in my old age. From my conversations with Ben, he seemed to want much the same things. He wanted to do things well, to enjoy himself, be loved by significant people, and be liked by people in general.

What I got, and what Ben was, in a sense, was a Blockhead. He had difficulty in most areas of his life. He had great charm, was sensitive and loving, but his illness and disabilities kept him from being able to function competently in many areas. But I feel Ben's suffering, like the son's suffering in The Golden Goose, was compensated by an inner treasury of eternal value.

If I could have been in charge of Ben's life, he would have lived for many years, free of problems of any kind. I wanted for Ben what most parents want for their children: to be happy, healthy, and prosperous. Instead, Ben was given hard tasks in life, a series of trials. Perhaps for Ben his task was to suffer and to travel inward. Blockheads may appear to the outer world as misfits, but to those who are looking at the mystery of life, no judgment is made. My son was wise beyond his years. His life played itself out according to its own unique plan.

In talking about my son I wish to take care not to eulogize him in such a way that his suicide is seen as a heroic act. I do not wish to inadvertently encourage more suicidal behavior. Dr. Garfinkle wrote in his book, Adolescent Suicide,

> "It is worth considering the effect of the increasing amount of attention society provides for suicide among the young. Suicide rates tend to correlate with the degree of social acceptance of suicidal behavior in particular cultures and sub-cultures (Hawton, 1986). It is quite likely that the heightened exposure in the media and in schools of both incidents and concerns about adolescent suicide is a double-edged sword. While it may increase sensitivity and responsiveness to a distressed adolescent, it may also serve to increase the acceptance and thereby the likelihood of suicide as an option of life's difficulties among such adolescents." (Hoberman, 1989, p. 18)

Instead of encouraging suicidal behavior, I wish to discourage it by describing how to discard inauthentic life (a life not in tune with your God-given talents, your authentic purpose) while choosing to continue living. People who do this end their old life **symbolically** and open themselves to their destiny. They do not literally commit suicide. They change.

Buckminster Fuller's Story

One person who came close to suicide but turned away was Buckminster Fuller. His life story offers an alternative to suicide. Mr. Fuller was a misfit, a failure, someone who had tragic losses early in life. He had decided to kill himself, but at the last moment did the kind of thinking that allowed him to change his life rather than destroy it.

Today, Buckminster Fuller is called "The Twentieth Century Leonardo da Vinci." But in 1927 he took a lonely walk by Lake Michigan with the intent of destroying himself. His brush with suicide, and the story of his early life is on the audio tape, The 50-Year Experiment. Married in 1917, he and his wife had their first child at the end of World War I. The little girl suffered spinal meningitis and infantile paralysis before her death at age four.

In the years after her death, Fuller plunged into work in the building trade. He constructed five small factories which made special building materials. He was interested in producing quality goods and in making buildings that would last. His products were used in the construction of 240 buildings on the East Coast. Fuller was not fundamentally interested in making money, and consequently, he did not. People backed him because he was bright, but he was in great disfavor for losing stockholders' money.

While Fuller was living in Chicago, penniless and disgraced, he felt confronted with an unsolvable financial dilemma. A second child was born during this time, and contemplating the fate of this healthy new child, Fuller felt the honorable thing for him to do was to commit suicide. He knew his mother and his in-laws would look after his wife and the new baby. He felt they could provide for them better than he could.

One windy night, Fuller left his apartment and walked by Lake Michigan with the intention of drowning himself. As he walked, he took stock of his life. His father died when Fuller was very young. His mother loved and doted on her son, but she did not understand his creative talents. She often admonished him by saying, "Never mind what you think, darling. Listen to those people who are trying to teach you." Consequently, Fuller did everything he could to learn what was being taught, even though much of it went against his creative intellect. To comply with his mother's wishes, he did the best he could to suppress his inner nature.

Now faced with the serious prospect of ending his life, Fuller weighed his options. He saw that during his 32 years he had always done what other people had told him to do, and all of that had come to naught. If he was going to continue, he would have to start fresh. "If I am going to do my own thinking, I must go entirely on experiential evidence; not on anything anyone told me to believe." (Fuller, 1983)

He then asked himself some fundamental questions: First, "is there a greater intelligence operating in the universe?" He believed that there was, and that the handiwork of that intelligence could be seen everywhere in, as he later put it, "the exquisite design of everything from the microcosm of atoms to the macromagnitudes of the galaxies" (Fuller, 1983).

He further asked himself: "Do I know best or does God know best whether I may be of any value to the universe?" He reasoned that his answer to the previous question, that there was a greater intelligence, implied what he called, "the apriori wisdom of the fact of your being." In other words, if there really is something big at work here, then there must be a good reason for your being here. But what was that good reason? The question remained: should he or should he not throw himself into the lake?

By now he was on to something. "You do not have the right to eliminate yourself," he thought. "You do not belong to you. You belong to the universe. Your significance will remain forever obscure to you, but you may assume that you are fulfilling your role if you apply yourself to converting your experience to the highest advantage of others." With that, Fuller had zeroed in on the premise of his life's work.

Motivated not by altruism but by a sincere and rational desire to discover empirically the operating principles of our world, he began his 50-year experiment to inventory those principles and share them with his fellow travelers on spaceship earth. The twin notions of a greater intelligence behind it all and a higher purpose for each individual in the cosmic evolutionary scheme are central to Fuller's philosophy, and stem from his inner dialogue in 1927.

More than 50 years later, in his book Critical Path, Fuller would equate evolution with the will of God, and say

"What I am trying to do is discover why God included humans in the universe. I am trying to find out....what God permits us progressively to know and preferably to do if we humans are to continue in the universe." So it could be said that according to Fuller, the tendency to concentrate on earning a living instead of pursuing one's natural curiosity about the mysteries of the universe is a kind of cosmic "putting the cart before the horse."

Having turned his back on the abyss, Fuller began his 50-year experiment that very night. Rather than committing suicide, he decided to put the horse before the cart; in fact, to lead an authentic life, in tune with his inner nature and the will of God.

> "I sought to use myself as my scientific guinea pig in a life-long experiment designed to discover what, if anything, a healthy young male of average size, experience, and capability, with an economically dependent wife and newborn child, starting without capital or any kind of wealth, cash savings, account money, credit or university degree, could effectively do that could improve the physical protection and support of all human lives and at the same time remove all undesirable restraints and improve individual initiative of any and all humans aboard our planet earth." (Fuller, Critical Path, 1983)

Fuller's goal was ambitious, befitting a man of his genius. Though we may not set goals as daunting for our own lives, we can go through a similar process. If a person's life is not working out, this is a signal for change. Fuller looked deep within himself and found what it was he really wanted to do. Joseph Campbell, eminent teacher and author, gives us exactly the same advice. He calls it "following your bliss." If we are to live an authentic life, we need to stop doing what other people tell us to do and start to look at what our inner wisdom tells us is our destiny.

Fuller's story is strikingly similar to the Blockhead tales. He too had painful experiences early in his life: the loss of his father, his school career which emphasized passive acceptance of existing assumptions (a system of education not well suited to the mind of a creative genius), the death of his first child, the disgrace of the loss of other people's money, his own destitution. At one of the most painful points of his life, he went inward, asking hard questions. "Do I know best, or does God know best whether I may be of any value to the universe?" Concluding that there was a design behind all things and a reason for the things that happen, he chose to devote his life to fulfilling his God-given assignment. Like Blockhead, Buckminster Fuller chose to live in accordance with an inner wisdom rather than satisfying the expectations of society.

According to Fuller's philosophy, no one has the right to eliminate themselves. We do not belong to ourselves; we belong to the universe. We will never completely know the meaning of our lives, but we can choose to convert our experiences to the highest advantage of others. By focusing on how we can use our experiences to help others and continue our struggles with life, we will live an authentic, noble life.

Chapter 5

Why Me?

When tragedy strikes, the questions arise: "Why is God doing this to me? Why have I been singled out for this? Have I done something bad that deserves punishment?" Rabbi Kushner's book, When Bad Things Happen to Good People, addresses this issue. I read it many years ago when dealing with another difficult situation. My husband and I were plagued by a business problem for a number of years. The problem we were having at that time is relevant here because the lessons I learned in dealing with that earlier problem helped me later to cope with the death of our son.

An earlier painful event in my life

Garry and I own and operate three small group homes for adults with mental retardation. When we entered this type of work in the late 1970's, we bought a facility for handicapped persons located in our own neighborhood. A year later we converted another house into a second group home. Three years later we attempted to build a new home for the retarded in a city about twenty miles away, where no other group home for the developmentally disabled had ever been available.

We bought two lots in a new subdivision so the house would have a big yard, and proceeded with our plans to build. Some of the neighbors in the area were concerned about the effect a group home would have on them. We tried to reassure them with facts (i.e., there was no evidence that the presence of a group home reduced property values or inhibited resale of other homes in the neighborhood.) We explained that group homes must be well maintained in order to meet federal and state regulations, so neighbors need not worry about the house becoming an eyesore. We informed the neighbors that they did not need to worry about the residents becoming a nuisance. Our clients are required by law to be well supervised, and involved in programs to enhance their skills. They would not just be hanging around the neighborhood with nothing to do. I told the neighbors we had recently built our own family home right next door to one of our group homes. Our actions proved our confidence in the facts about these group homes, as they exist in our particular state. If there were any reason to feel that a group home would have a negative impact on neighbors, we certainly would not have built our family home right next to one.

We went through a number of meetings and procedures where these issues were discussed over and over again. Some of the neighbors remained unconvinced. After many months we finally were given permission to proceed. At this point a few of the neighbors went to court and got a temporary restraining order to restrict the placement of the house on the lot. The home we had hoped to complete in September was left waiting in the factory all fall and winter. The legal process took many turns, and the neighbors ultimately took the case to the Minnesota State Supreme Court, where we once again received approval for the project.

The emotional toll was great. The whole situation seemed a waste in so many ways. All of the time and energy I was using to work on this problem could have been used to do something more constructive. It was also a waste of the neighbors' time and energy. They too could have been using their resources to pursue something that would have benefited them rather than interfering with our project. Legal fees and added construction costs meant financial losses for us. The neighbors probably also had legal fees to pay. At the time, all I could say was, "What a waste!"

Is it only bad luck?

It was at this time I read Rabbi Kushner's book. This book is helpful to people who tend to feel guilty about the bad things that happen to them. Some people think God judges us for past deeds and doles out punishment to fit the crime; Kushner's book provides a different perspective. He asserts the position that tragedies are not a punishment for past deeds, they are simply misfortune.

Where does the erroneous assumption that connects tragedy with guilt come from? Dr. Lionnel Corbett, a psychiatrist with a strong interest in spirituality, explains why some people think they deserve the bad things that happen to them. Corbett says that we have been taught God is our

Father. If we project onto God our experience with our earthly father, we will assume that God acts as our earthly father would act. For example, as children our parents punished us when we did something wrong. The punishment is perceived by children as deserved, as a natural consequence of misdeeds. If we project onto our heavenly Father assumptions about divine motivations that reflect experiences with earthly parents, we assume the Divine thinks and acts like an earthly father would. Projection of human behavior onto God fails to make a distinction between Divine perspective and human thought.

To interpret tragedies as punishment is inaccurate for two reasons. First, it is unlikely the Divine mind conforms to our human thinking. We have no way of knowing what is in the mind of God, but it is unlikely that God has the same perspective as ours. A familiar New Testament story of suffering illustrates my point:

> And as Jesus passed by, he saw a man which was blind from his birth. And his disciples asked him, saying, Master, who did sin, this man, or his parents, that he was born blind? Jesus answered, Neither hath this man sinned, nor his parent; but that the works of God should be made manifest in him. (John 9: 45)

Jesus makes it clear that illnesses and genetic conditions are not punishments for past sins. They are necessary suffering to fulfill the purpose of the person's life.

Second, any interpretation of our current suffering as resulting from some past deed is backward thinking.

Interpreting the bad things that are happening to you as exclusively the result of an indiscretion in your past ignores the importance of the future. Dr. Corbett emphasizes that the painful events in life may have vital implication for our future. He, like others interested in Jungian psychology, upholds that what happens now (painful as it is) may be necessary for some future challenge. The difficult situation you are currently facing may serve as preparation for something yet to come.

A forward perspective ties into my sense of the purpose behind the suffering I experienced when we built our group home. Our earlier painful experience prepared me for what was to come. My perception of what it taught me is this: During the two to three years we struggled with that house, it was extremely important for me to learn how to conduct myself in a calm, reasonable, and nonvindictive manner over an extended period of time. The building of the group home was covered by the local news media. I needed to develop the skill of handling myself while in the public eye.

As I anguished over the sheer waste of time and energy the interference with our project caused everyone, I grew in my faith that those frustrations would be of use to me in the future. I had no idea why I was being taught the skills I was learning or what I was being prepared for. I only came to believe there was a purpose for it all, some ultimate benefit.

Seeing a theme running through one's life

I can now see how those lessons many years ago help me today in a number of ways. First, Ben's death as a result of suicide and the period of grief which followed was another time I needed to conduct myself in a calm, reasonable, and nonvindictive way over an extended period of time. Ben's death was no one's fault. Anger is a natural part of the grief process. I was incredibly angry, but that earlier training allowed me to develop skills to cope with my anger. Second, my willingness to share information about Ben's life and death comes partly from that time when our family business caused us to feel as if we were living in a goldfish bowl. Last, the anguish over the loss of our boy, in whom we poured hours of time and energy to help him learn how to cope with life, was monumental when compared to the frustration over the wasted time and energy spent on building delays. All of our efforts to teach him coping skills were not a waste because our efforts had lasting value for him and for us. What do any of us take with us when we die, if not the experiences that produce personal/spiritual growth?

Rabbi Kushner encourages people not to feel guilty about the bad things that happen. Jungian psychology differs from Kushner's stance in that it invests meaning in these painful occurrences. Most people do ask, "Why is this happening to me?" It is only natural to look for meaning during tragedy. Asking "Why me?" is not a waste of time. Some deep instinct, some inner wisdom, tells us to look for the meaning. This is where faith is important. One's faith lies in the belief that what is happening serves a higher purpose. Some day we will understand what that purpose is.

I believe people who ask, “Why is God doing this to me?” should be encouraged to continue to ask themselves this question, but do so in a way that allows them to be nonjudgmental. A caring person can gently point out to a person in distress that the Divine is not acting like a punishing parent in presenting them with suffering, but that their pain does have some important meaning. Difficult situations do have a goal which only time will reveal.

Dr. Corbett states that looking ahead to the future rather than to the past helps change a person's perspective on suffering. Having faith that there is some meaning to suffering helps to alleviate the pain. And when a person is finally able to discover the meaning of what happened, healing takes place. Jung had this to say about suffering: "The only thing that frees you is meaning. Science and common sense don't provide any answers to the problem of suffering." (Jaffe, 1963). Science and common sense can not approach the question most frequently asked by people in pain: "Why me?"

Dr. Viktor Frankl, the Viennese psychiatrist, developed a system of therapy focused on finding meaning during difficult life circumstances. Frankl (1959) encourages people to use painful times for growth.

> “Whenever one is confronted with an inescapable, unavoidable situation, whenever one has to face a fate that cannot be changed, e.g., an incurable disease, such

> as an inoperable cancer, just then is one given a last chance to actualize the highest value, to fulfill the deepest meaning, the meaning of suffering. For what matters above all is the attitude we take toward suffering, the attitude in which we take our suffering upon ourselves."

One of his famous cases describes how Dr. Frankl's therapy helps to relieve suffering through the process of honoring it.

> "Once, an elderly general practitioner consulted me because of his severe depression. He could not overcome the loss of his wife who had died two years before and whom he had loved above all else. Now how could I help him? What should I tell him? Well, I refrained from telling him anything, but instead confronted him with the question, 'What would have happened, Doctor, if you had died first, and your wife would have had to survive you?' 'Oh,' he said, 'for her this would have been terrible; how she would have suffered!' Whereupon I replied, 'You see, Doctor, such a suffering has been spared her, and it is you who have spared her this suffering; but now, you have to pay for it by surviving and mourning her.' He said no word but shook my hand and calmly left my office." (Frankl, 1959 p. 178-179)

Frankl goes on, "Suffering ceases to be suffering in some way at the moment it finds a meaning, such as the meaning of a sacrifice." (Frankl, 1959 p. 178-179). The general practitioner in the story saw a meaning to his grief and viewed it as an heroic act. In so doing, the meaning serves to eliminate unnecessary suffering.

Jung said, "Meaning makes a great many things endurable, perhaps everything." (Jaffe, 1963) No one knows for certain if meaning has the ability to make everything bearable, but finding a personal meaning does make tragedies more tolerable. In doing therapy with people who suffer, Dr. Corbett states that the doctor "has to help the person find the meaning that quickens or that enlivens." This implies that the meaning people discover is tailor-made for their own particular dilemma. It is an individualized answer, not a generalized truism. Frankl's example demonstrates this beautifully. He helped this elderly physician find the meaning that was most relevant for his situation. The unavoidable suffering of the client then takes on a new perspective.

This new perspective is multi-dimensional. Dr. Corbett states, "If you discover the meaning, you can objectify the situation. You can get some distance from the situation, some perspective and not identify with it so much." Any change in the way the suffering is interpreted only occurs when the individual is ready to discover meaning. Individual readiness needs to be respected. For example, some people grieve their loss for an extensive period of time, where other people have a shorter grieving period. It is important for all of us to respect individual differences. But it is especially helpful to anyone whose job involves work with the bereaved to have insights into these individual differences.

Relating personal themes to ancient patterns

When people suffer a tragedy, the meaning of their suffering and the severity of their pain is based, to some extent, on the archetype that dominates their personality. Jung described archetypes as forces within the minds of each person. Archetypes are universal patterns in the psyche which influence how we think and behave. Although all of us have the same patterns in our psyche, each person will be influenced more by some of these archetypes than by others. The particular effect these patterns have on each of us explains our individual differences.

One way to learn about the archetypes of the psyche is to become familiar with ancient Greek stories. The Greeks honored the archetypes in their tales of the gods and goddesses. For example, the feminine archetypes dominant in many personalities are personified by these Greek goddesses. The stories of the following three goddesses illustrate how the feminine aspect of the psyche may react to loss.

DEMETER , the Mother

The Greek goddess Demeter, the Earth Mother, ruled over all of nature, protecting young, defenseless creatures. Demeter produced the abundance of the earth, and each summer the people offered thanks to her for the bounty. Presiding over the birth of new life, Demeter ruled over the orderly cycles of nature. She is the image of the power within the earth itself. It is said that she taught men how to plow and till the soil and taught women how to grind wheat and bake bread.

Demeter loved her only daughter, Persephone. One day their happy life was violently changed when Persephone went out for a walk and did not return. For years Demeter searched everywhere for her beloved daughter, but Persephone had vanished without a trace. Years later, word came of Persephone's fate. Hades, the dark lord of the underworld, had abducted her.

Enraged over her loss, Demeter allowed the earth to go barren. Persephone was now queen of the underworld, but Demeter could not accept the change. Hades treated Persephone with honor; she, in turn, ate the pomegranate, the fruit of the underworld.

In her grief Demeter refused to function as the goddess of bounty. The whole of mankind was in danger of perishing from lack of food. Eventually, a compromise was reached. For nine months of every year, Persephone lived with her mother on earth. The other three months each year Persephone returned to her husband in the underworld.

Even this solution was difficult for Demeter to bear. Each year when Persephone went away, the Earth Mother went into mourning, causing flowers to wither, trees to lose their leaves, and the earth to grow barren and cold. Each year, when her daughter returned in spring, fertility returned to the earth.

For any mother who has Demeter as the dominant archetype in her personality, the loss of a child is the ultimate tragedy. Like Demeter, such a woman may never come to terms with her loss. Others, seeing the extensive bereavement of a Demeter-dominated mother, will understand her better when they understand this archetypal pattern and see how it dominates the woman's personality. The woman may also begin to understand herself and respect her inability to come to terms with her loss. An appreciation of this story provides some meaning for the suffering she continues to endure if she understands how the archetype dominates her individual psyche.

A woman with a strong Demeter force has great difficulty coming to terms with the loss of a child, but she may be able to accept the loss of her husband. This does not mean her spouse was not loved greatly. It simply implies the difference in the strength of one archetype in her particular personality. Compare this with a woman for whom Hera is predominant.

HERA, the Wife

The ancient Greeks honored Hera as the powerful goddess of marriage. One of the Olympian goddesses, Hera was the wife of Zeus, the chief god. The Hera archetype represents a woman's longing to be a wife.

> "A woman with a strong Hera archetype feels fundamentally incomplete without a partner. She is motivated by a 'goddess-given' instinct toward marriage. Her grief at being without a mate can be as deep and wounding an inner experience as being childless is for a woman whose strongest urge is to have a baby. ...When Hera is her archetype, a bride may feel like a goddess on her wedding day. For her, impending marriage evokes the anticipation of fulfillment and completeness, which fills her with joy. ...The Hera archetype provides the capacity to bond, to be loyal and faithful, to endure difficulties with a partner. When Hera is a motivating force, the woman's commitment is not conditional. Once married, she means to stay so, for better or worse." (Bolen, 1984, p. 142-144)

Although the loss of a child would be extremely painful for a woman who is dominated by the Hera archetype, she would likely be able to come to terms with it. The loss of a spouse will be a tragedy of enormous magnitude for the Hera-dominated woman. Dr. Jean Bolen, (1984, p.154) Jungian analyst and author of Goddesses in Every Woman, writes that for a Hera dominated woman, being a wife is her primary role. "The bond to her husband is her major source of meaning." She may feel empty and incomplete as a widow. Her life may appear over, and life alone is empty and meaningless. Added to this is the fact that many of her activities revolve around herself and her husband as a couple interacting with other couples. She is likely to lose her social support once she becomes a single person. For the Hera dominated woman, widowhood is a double loss: she lost the person that needed and loved her, the person who gave her life meaning, but she also lost her social network, finding herself very much alone once she no longer fits into her former friendships made up of married couples. The Hera dominated woman sometimes does not have close friendships with other women, a valuable resource for any single woman.

Vulnerable versus Virgin Goddesses

Dr. Bolen's work on feminine archetypes led her to describe both the Demeter and Hera patterns as vulnerable goddesses. Grieving people who have one of these patterns as the dominant theme of their lives are vulnerable to an enormous amount of unavoidable pain following a loss. Knowledge of the goddess patterns can help to objectify their situation.

They are functioning like Demeter or like Hera. They can not expect themselves to feel or act any differently. Once they honor the goddess pattern within them, they can gain an objective perspective of their situation. They may be ready to begin to appreciate other goddess patterns; the virgin goddesses. Cultivating these archetypes which also exist in their psyche can be helpful to women dominated by vulnerable archetypes. Deliberate work to develop those less powerful forces within the psyche of a vulnerable personality serves to ease the pain of the loss and reduce unnecessary suffering.

Bolen (1984, p.36) describes the virgin goddesses as patterns of being feminine in which the woman is one-in-herself. A virgin pattern in a woman means "she will be motivated by a need to follow her own inner values, to do what has meaning or fulfills herself, apart from what other people think. ... The virgin goddess aspect is the true essence of who the woman is and of what she values."

ARTEMIS, independent spirituality

In sharp contrast to the vulnerable patterns of Demeter (mother) and Hera (wife) is the virgin goddess Artemis, Goddess of the Hunt and Goddess of the Moon. "As Goddess of the Hunt, dressed in a short tunic, armed with a silver bow, a quiver of arrows on her back, she was the archer with unerring aim. As Goddess of the Moon, she is also shown as a lightbearer, carrying torches in her hands, or with the moon and stars surrounding her head." (Bolen, 1984, p. 46)

Artemis personifies an independent feminine spirit.

"The archetype she represents enables a woman to seek her own goals on terrain of her own choosing. ...The Artemis archetype gives a woman the innate ability to concentrate intensely on whatever is important to her and to be undistracted from her course, either by the needs of

> others or by competition from others." (Bolen, 1984, p. 49)

The Artemis archetype represents "achievement and competence, independence from men and male opinions." (Bolen, 1984, p. 50) She values friendships with men, but strives to excel in what she does because of her own reasons, not primarily to please a man, to gain his approval or to elicit praise. Bolen describes the importance that friendships with other women have for the Artemis woman. These strong friendships often last for decades and provide a support network. Here is a place to share their greatest joys and their deepest sorrows. It is within these friendships that the Artemis in everyone gets the help needed to solve problems, as well as receive the ordinary, everyday companionship from someone of the same sex which makes life less lonely.

The Artemis woman who chooses to become a mother is often a good one. The symbol of this archetype is the bear. As such, she is a powerful protector of the young (in fact, of all who are in need of protection), but not overly protective. Bolen writes that she is the type of mother who "fosters independence, who teaches her young how to fend for themselves. ...Artemis mothers do not look back with longing to when their children were babies or dependent toddlers. Instead, they look forward to when their children will be more independent." (Bolen, 1984, p.64)

The description of Artemis as a bereaved mother, and her concern for victimized, powerless children gives a different perspective than the Demeter mother. The Artemis woman can come to terms with the loss of the child, but may be haunted when contemplating the suffering the child went through while alive. The focus of her grief is more on the painful life the child led than on the death.

In the second half of life, the woman dominated by the Artemis archetype becomes like the Goddess of the Moon. The focus is now on spirituality. If an Artemis-dominated woman experiences a loss, she can feel comforted by thoughts of the spiritual nature of all people. The Artemis-type woman will find meaning in her spirituality. She remembers everyone's basic nature is spiritual, even when alive. She will not feel totally unconnected to the spirit of the loved one who has gone into the spiritual realm. The Artemis-dominated woman may come to genuinely feel she has not really lost the loved one. The spiritual connection remains.

Deep friendships and meaningful work are important to the Artemis-dominated person. Women can be encouraged to do meaningful work and to strengthen their existing friendships in order to reduce unnecessary suffering. Women dominated by the vulnerable goddesses -- Demeter, the Earth Mother, and Hera, the goddess of marriage, can continue to honor these archetypes while they begin to cultivate virgin patterns like Artemis.

On a personal level, I am dominated by the Artemis archetype. Ben's sudden death, like all sudden deaths, created a long period of grief. Two to three years is a fairly typical length for grief of the sudden loss of a child. As an Artemis woman I ultimately came to terms with my loss. I have often said I was less upset thinking about my son's death than thinking of the enormous pain he went through while he was alive. This statement is what one would expect from a person dominated by an archetype concerned with the victimized, the powerless, and the young.

In middle age, Artemis functions as Goddess of the Moon. When Ben died I found comfort in the words of a Native American chant: "I am spirit, spirit am I." Those words reminded me of our essential nature. My son was now in spirit. Our connection was not broken.

I do not interpret my son's condition as a punishment for something he had done or as a punishment for some sin I had committed. What both of us suffered was necessary for the fulfillment of the purpose of our lives. This is where faith is essential. I do not need to have faith that there is a God. My experience tells me there is a Divine force in the universe. My faith lies in a belief that there is a purpose, a meaning to suffering, and that suffering serves some future goal.

When trying to discover a personal meaning for our tragedy, knowledge of the archetypes can be helpful. The archetypes provide a perspective which objectifies the pain and it facilitates a broader meaning. Objectifying the grief of any loss allows the sufferer more distance from it.

Chapter 6

Seeking Meaning

My faith in the value of suffering was inspired by Dr. Viktor Frankl's classic, Man's Search for Meaning. Loved by millions who read it, Frankl's book describes his experience as a prisoner in Hitler's concentration camps.

The Story of Viktor Frankl

Frankl lost his father, his mother, his brother, and his wife. Of his entire family, only he and his sister escaped death. Like everyone sent to the concentration camps, Frankl was stripped of all his worldly possessions. He suffered from hunger, cold, and brutality. He lived with the realization that at any hour he could be summoned for extermination. If anyone is in a position to take a wise and compassionate stance in relationship to the meaning of suffering, he is. Dr. Frankl's ideas ring true because they are based on experience.

The essence of Dr. Frankl's teaching is that everyone who lives suffers; those people who find the means to survive accomplish this by finding a meaning in their suffering. For if there is any purpose at all in life then there must be some purpose in suffering and in death. But no one can tell anyone else what this purpose is. Every person must find his own meaning for himself, and needs to accept the responsibility his unique answer prescribes.

Frankl's twin notions of finding meaning and acting responsibly to fulfill the purpose behind the suffering are what gives life nobility. His respect for meaning and willingness to act in accordance with a higher meaning began long before he entered the camps. In the late 1930's, as the threat of Nazism loomed heavily in the countries near Germany, Dr. Frankl faced the dilemma of whether to leave Austria or to stay. He and his wife wanted to leave, but his parents would not go. He could not decide which was best -- to leave his parents behind or to stay with them. Out for a walk one day, struggling with this decision, he came upon a fragment of an engraved stone. On it was inscribed a part of the fourth commandment: Honor thy father and thy mother. Frankl took this coincidence as a meaningful sign he should stay in Austria with his parents. Coincidences such as these are clues to the course one's life is meant to take.

Late one night the Gestapo came to get him and his family. Allowed to take only a few possessions, Frankl took the manuscript he had been working on for years. Soon even this was confiscated. Stripped of his life's work, Frankl came to understand that he must live the thesis of his book; namely, the pain in life can be endured if there is meaning. Frankl (1959, p. 121) is fond of quoting Nietzsche: "He who has a why to live can bear with almost any how."

Life in the camps seemed unendurable, but according to Frankl, those who possessed what he termed "a will to meaning" found it possible to survive. He discovered it was even possible to find a measure of freedom as a prisoner. The last human freedom always remains, regardless of the circumstances: the ability to choose the *attitude* in any situation. Prison is an opportunity to look inward, to grow. Not everyone who is given the opportunity to grow through suffering accepts the challenge to open up spiritually. Frankl made it clear not everyone chose a positive direction. Some prisoners became more negative during their stay in the concentration camps. Their desire to live and the fear of death made them even more egocentric than ever.

Suffering is a call to explore more deeply the nature of one's own being. Frankl described the spiritual growth that occurred in some of the inmates. He wrote how sensitive people (those with a rich inner life) suffer pain, but their inner selves may not experience much damage. Although they often had delicate constitutions, they had the ability to retreat mentally from their terrible conditions and go inward to a life of inner beauty and spiritual freedom. These prisoners, who were less physically fit, sometimes survived the rigors of camp better than those with a more robust nature.

Most of us have read or were told stories about what life in the concentration camps was like. Each day, in the freezing winter, in the rains of spring, and in the heat of summer, prisoners had to work outdoors clothed only in rags. One icy day, as Frankl marched for miles to his work site, a comment from a fellow prisoner triggered the memory of his beloved wife. Dirty and in rags, his fellow inmate said, if our wives could only see us now! That simple comment transfixed him. Under those horrible conditions Frankl saw the beauty of meaning described by poets and proclaimed as the ultimate wisdom by philosophers: the truth that love is indeed the final and highest goal to which anyone can aspire. The moment produced a spiritual revelation: any person's salvation lies through love and in love. He then realized that people who lost everything can still know bliss, even if it is only for a minute, as they remember their beloved. In a time of utter desolation, when they cannot express themselves through positive action, when their only achievement consists of enduring suffering in the best way -- the honorable way -- in such a circumstance, people can, through loving remembrance of their beloved, achieve fulfillment. For the first time in his life Frankl truly understood the meaning of the phrase, "The angels were lost in perpetual contemplation of an infinite glory."

With this spiritual revelation, Frankl understood that love goes beyond the mere physical existence of the person. Love finds its genuine meaning in the spiritual being of the inner self. Whether or not a person is actually present, or even alive at all, stops being important.

Frankl had no way of knowing whether his wife was dead or alive. At the moment of his revelation it ceased to matter. There was no need to know, because nothing could alter the power of his love or the memory of his beloved.

When any of us compare our lives to Frankl's, we may momentarily feel ashamed of the self pity we experience with our own suffering, but Frankl himself would not minimize our problems. He points out that no matter what the cause of our pain or the size of our loss, any suffering is important because it tends to fill us completely. He compares suffering to the behavior of a gas. When a quantity of gas is put into an empty container, it fills it up completely and evenly, no matter how big the container is. Likewise, suffering completely fills a person's soul and mind, regardless if the problem is actually great or small.

On a personal level, I find truth in Frankl's beliefs. Little disappointments can absolutely ruin my day, and as Frankl implies, the everyday painful frustrations do have the potential to allow me to grow. Whether or not we use life's difficulties as opportunities for spiritual growth is a matter of choice. Sometimes it is also a matter of how much energy we have at the time to cope. Frankl readily admits that he had many opportunities to be of help to others in the concentration camp, but the stress of overwork, malnutrition, and the seemingly overwhelming nature of the situation often prevented him from doing so.

Suffering always brings up the questions, "Why is God doing this to me? What does God want me to do? What is my destiny?" Even when the meaning of pain cannot be deciphered, the person who believes that whatever he experiences is destiny will find some peace of mind. He may then be saved from the torture of regretting a road not taken.

Respect for destiny, the dominance of the will of God over the will of man, is a frequent theme in stories. It appeared in "The Three Feathers" when the king sent each son to go the direction the wind blew their feather. Frankl underscored the importance of unavoidable destiny in the following story.

Death in Teheran

A wealthy and powerful Persian was walking in his garden along with a servant. The servant cried out that he just met Death, who threatened him. He implored his master to lend him a fast horse so he could escape Death by going to Teheran. The servant was sure that he could get there that very night. The master granted the request and the servant left immediately. When the master returned to his home, he himself met Death. He asked, "Why did you frighten my servant and threaten him?" To which Death replied, "I did not threaten him; I was just surprised to find him here when I planned to meet him tonight in Teheran."

Unlike the servant in the "Death In Teheran," the unpredictability of camp life caused many of Frankl's fellow captives to avoid making decisions. Instead, they developed a faith in destiny. They grew to have a strong belief that fate was their master. They believed one should not influence what happened to them, but let destiny take its own course. Like the king in the story of "The Three Feathers," these prisoners of the concentration camps had the sense something other than their conscious minds were in charge of their lives. They were willing to put themselves in the hands of their destiny and endure suffering with dignity.

Using meaning to transcend tragedy

We have all known people who suffcr with dignity. We have seen how sometimes the worst circumstances brings out the best in some people. Frankl saw how the concentration camp experience produced heroes. Some inmates were able to suppress the irritability that malnutrition, overwork, and deprivation produces. Camp survivors remember heroes who comforted others and gave away their last bit of food. These heroes were few, but their examples offer proof that everything can be stripped from a person except one thing. The final human freedom is the ability to choose one's own way. A famous poet once wrote: "Stone walls do not a prison make, nor iron bars a cage." Frankl affirms that freedom exists in any situation, once individuals realize they are free.

Everyone can choose what shall become of them -- mentally and spiritually. They can retain dignity even in the worst of circumstances. It is spiritual freedom, something which cannot be taken away, that makes life meaningful and purposeful. It is the way people accept their fate, including suffering, which gives deep meaning to life.

In order to achieve something with suffering, it is essential to believe that what is happening is important and that every life is important. If one defines important people as those who possess power, wealth, beauty, or talent, one misses the point that all of us are children of God. **Each of us lives a life that is a sacred story.** When we see our lives as sacred, then the powerful events, especially painful ones, take on significance and meaning. Frankl wrote that everyone confronts fate; everyone has a chance to achieve something through suffering. Those who get stuck in self-pity miss the opportunity to grow spiritually beyond themselves. The people who fail to use times of difficult external circumstances fail the greatest test of life. Frankl wrote that rather than taking the camp's hardships as a test of inner strength, these people failed to take life seriously. They hated this greatest life challendge, and dismissed it as of no consequence. They closed their eyes to what was before them and lived only in the past. Current life for those people was meaningless.

An approach that looks forward, rather than backward, is essential for survival. Frankl's camp experience taught him that when inmates lost faith in the future they were doomed. If they lost belief in their personal future, they lost their spiritual hold. Once this happened they declined and became susceptible to mental and physical deterioration.

Frankl tells us how a forward-looking attitude is necessary to maintain the will to live. He recalled two cases of suicide. Both persons talked of their intentions to die. Both gave the same reason, which was that they expected nothing more from life. Frankl knew that in both cases it was essential to help them realize that life still expected something from them.

Two things are necessary in helping someone in tragic circumstances. The first is to assist the person in paying attention to what is significant in their life. The second is the need to focus on action. What is needed is a basic change of attitude toward life. We need to learn it ourselves, and then teach others that it does not matter what we expect from our lives, but what life expects from us. Instead of aimlessly asking, "What is the meaning of life?," it is helpful to think of what life is asking us to do every day and every hour. What is important for us to do? Answers consist not in vague talk, but in positive action. Ultimately, life involves taking responsibility for finding the right answer to our problems and fulfilling the tasks life continually sets for each person.

A particular task, the meaning of one's life, differs not only from person to person, but also from one moment to the next. "Life does not mean something philosophical, but something realistic and specific, just as life's challenges are very real. They consist of everyone's destiny, which is different for each person. No one can be compared to another and no one's destiny can be compared to anyone else's. Every situation is unique and requires a different response."

Frankl's assertions are the same wisdom found in fairy tales. Life presents us with tasks. They may seem impossible; they are often painful, and they form our destiny. The tasks change from one stage to another and each person must go his or her own direction.

Frankl taught that meaning comes from different sources, and everyone needs to find meaning in their own way. There is no universal answer, no 100% effective prescription that produces a meaningful life or heals all tragedies. We have to find our own way. For many people, the source of life's meaning comes from loving relationships with family and friends.

When it is impossible to replace a loved one, Frankl maintains that the task of those who are left to grieve is to realize that something is still expected of them in their ongoing relationship with the deceased. It consists of something in the future that they alone can do.

For other people or at other times, life's meaning is found in creative work. Meaningful work allows the expression of uniqueness. An unfinished task that only he can perform gives one a strong hold on life. Frankl believed that a sense of responsibility towards the completion of important work will deter the sufferer from destroying his life. He stresses that anyone who knows a 'why' for existence can bear almost any circumstance.

Throughout his writing, Frankl continued to emphasize the value of suffering for the growth of the personality. As painful as suffering is, it can be embraced. Citing Nietcha's: 'that which does not kill me, makes me stronger,' Frankl says,"In the final analysis, one has to decide whether or not to take life seriously enough to embrace the growth that can come from suffering." (Frankl, 1959)

Frankl taught that if people learn it is their destiny to suffer, they will accept the suffering as their task. In suffering each of us is

> "unique and alone in the universe. ...No one can relieve another of his suffering or suffer in his place. Every person's unique opportunity lies specifically in the way he chooses to bear his burden. ... If there is a meaning in life at all, then there must be a meaning in suffering. Suffering is an inevitable part of life, even as fate and death. Without suffering and death, human life cannot be complete." (Frankl, 1959)

Chapter 7

Spiritual Development

I am a very practical, businesslike person. I invested a lot in my son, trying every way I knew to help him make his life 'work.' If the return on my investment is just the box of ashes our family took home after cremation, then I really was cheated. In one respect, it seemed as if a dirty trick was being played on me. But the premise of this book is that suffering is of value. I now ask, "How can the enormous pain I have gone through since his death bring about my own growth?" This chapter begins to address this question. In order to see where Ben's death took me in my spiritual growth, I need to start by describing my spiritual perspective before Ben's death.

Childhood Spiritual Roots

My childhood, in the second half of the 1940's and in the 1950's, was steeped in the rich tradition of the Latin Mass of the Catholic church. The many rituals of church provided me with an appreciation of symbolism pointing to the mystery beyond what can be understood. The Latin mass gave an opportunity for interior (inner) experience. It created an environment in which meditation and contemplation were possible.

I am not the only one who acknowledges the spiritual, mystical benefit of ritual, the Latin mass, and the liturgical year. Joseph Campbell, a prominent authority on the power of myths, recalls his own Catholic upbringing. He says,

> "Now, one of the great advantages of being brought up as a Roman Catholic is that you're taught to take myth seriously and to let it operate on your life and to live in terms of these mythic motifs. I was brought up in terms of the seasonal relationships to the cycle of Christ's coming into the world, teaching in the world, dying, resurrecting, and returning to heaven. The ceremonies all through the year keep you in mind of the eternal core of all that changes in time. Sin is simply getting out of touch with that harmony." (Flowers, 1988, p. 10)

Like Campbell, I respect the value of ritual and myth. Religion has been an important ingredient in my life. My parents were very religious people, and we were raised to attend church at almost every opportunity. During my eight years of elementary education I attended our local parochial school. This meant I would begin each morning by attending Mass. During the academic year I attended Mass each day except Saturday. Besides Mass, there were various prayer services which we attended at least once a week.

In addition to attending church, our family said the rosary at home each evening after dinner. Saying the rosary is a very disciplined activity. Some people may not see the value of saying a prayer over and over again. When you say a rosary you disengage from daily concerns and turn inward; you concentrate on the inner dimension. Many people find it beneficial to routinely practice some kind of meditative exercise twenty minutes each day, approximately the same amount of time it takes to say a rosary.

My family was what Joseph Campbell would describe as "substantial Catholics." In the PBS production of The Hero's Journey, he described his own similar upbringing:

> "Born in(to) an Irish Catholic family and environment and spending your boyhood with nuns and serving Mass as a little altar boy...you are studying the Catholic doctrine all the time with a deep belief. I think anyone who wasn't Catholic in that substantial way has no realization of the ambiance of religion within which you live. It is potent, it is life supporting, and it is beautiful."

When I was about five years old, I had an experience of spiritual revelation. It is my belief that many, if not most people, encounter these events but they may not pay attention to them and thus do not think of themselves as having a religious experience. My experience is not noteworthy because it was unusual. It is just that as with dreams, I pay attention to the small but very meaningful inner events of my life.

One sunny day when I was five or six years old, I was sitting near a window. As the sunshine streamed through the window and hit my body, I experienced this realization: "For the time that I was on earth I would have this body. Before I was born, I was only spirit, and after I died I would again return to spirit. But for the time I was on earth I had a body." This was not a revelation which produced either fear or joy; it was simply an experience of very deep knowledge which has stayed with me all of my life and has been very meaningful to me. I do not recall if I told anyone about it. Like most children, I realized adults do not often take seriously what children say. This revelation did not contradict anything I had been taught; it merely affirmed it in a very deep level.

I had a typical formal Catholic education in the parochial schools of the 1950's. Catechism was taught along with reading, writing, and arithmetic. It consisted of memorizing the answers to various religious questions. One of the questions I remembered learning was: "How do we know that Jesus was the one and only son of God?" The answer we memorized was, "We know that Jesus was the one and only son of God because he died and arose from the dead." This supplied our proof that Christianity was the one and only "correct" religion.

During those elementary school years and well into high school, I felt no need to question my religious beliefs. When I attended college, however, the world opened up for me. In my freshman year I had a World History class. Much to the credit of my history professor, he felt a nation's religious beliefs were as much a legitimate subject for study as the stories of their wars. One of these stories was the Egyptian tale of Osiris and Isis. This story was pivotal to the questioning of my religious beliefs, and probably exemplified the type of experience most young people go through. This religious myth is worth retelling.

The Story of the Egyptian God Osiris

Osiris was the king of Egypt and Isis was his queen. Wise, kindly Osiris showed the people of his country how to grow crops. He was the giver of laws and taught the Egyptians how to worship the gods. His brother, Seth, was jealous of Osiris and plotted against him. At a banquet, Seth spoke of a splendid chest he had made. Seth promised to give it to anyone who could fit into it exactly. All the other guests tried and failed. As Osiris got into the chest, Seth signaled his fellow conspirators. They slammed the lid of the chest down, bolted it tight, and sealed it with molten lead.

The chest became Osiris' coffin and was carried to the bank of the Nile. The conspirators dumped it into the water, hoping it would be lost forever. Seth then became the new king.

When Isis learned of her husband's death, she was grief stricken. She went to search for the coffin, which had drifted ashore and attached itself to a young tree. The sapling grew into a tall, graceful tree in a single night. When the king of that region heard of this miraculous tree, he sent workmen to cut it down to become a pillar in his palace.

Isis came to this kingdom and in time became a trusted servant in the royal household. Each evening as the rest of the palace slept, Isis went to the room containing the pillar, and wept at her husband's coffin. During the daytime she cared for the baby prince. Isis grew to love the infant. Deciding to make him immortal, she took him one night to the room containing the pillar. She kindled a fire, whispered a spell over the baby, and placed the sleeping infant in the flames. The fire would burn away the baby's humanity.

The noise of the crackling of flames awoke the queen. She screamed in horror when she saw the infant prince. The baby was rescued from the magic flames. Isis told the queen who she was and regretfully told her that her little son would now never be immortal.

Weeping at her mistake, the queen asked how she could now serve the goddess. Isis requested that the pillar housing the body of Osiris be removed. It was plucked as easy as a flower from under the roof. Isis was given their finest boat and a crew to sail it. With the coffin aboard, Isis traveled to the marshes of Egypt.

One evening as Isis slept, Seth came hunting in those marshes and came upon the coffin. Recognizing it, he opened the coffin, lifted his brother's corpse, and tore it into bits. He scattered the pieces throughout the kingdom, hoping Isis would not find them all. When Isis discovered the emptied coffin, her cries reached the heavens. Nephthys, her sister, quickly came to help her. For many long years, devoted Isis and kindly Nephthys roamed throughout Egypt in search of the pieces of Osiris' body. Finally, they managed to gather them all and put them together. Isis then worked her greatest miracle. As the two goddesses took the form of hawks, they watched over the body, covering it with their wings, and Isis prayed that her husband would be restored.

She managed to revive Osiris for one night, wherein a promised child was conceived. Following that one night, even though Osiris was dead, his spirit lived on. Ra-Atum made Osiris the King of the Dead, ruling the Realm of the Beautiful West. From that time on, Egyptians knew that death was nothing to fear, because their spirit would live on in the Kingdom of Osiris.

Questioning the Existence of God

My reading of this story of Osiris and Isis was my first encounter with other gods who died and arose from the dead. Christians were not the first people to believe in a resurrected god who afterwards ruled as King of the afterlife. For me, the Catholic catechism's teachings were shattered. I spent the next ten years questioning my beliefs. Was there really some sort of external God, or were we just kidding ourselves? Karl Marx and Sigmund Freud asserted, though from differing premises, that human beings invent religions to make themselves feel better. Is religion only an "opiate of the masses," nothing but defenses in times of tragedy to soften the reality of our own mortality?

If one is inclined to think God does not exist; God is merely an invention of human thought, then there is no end to explanations for how people invent God. Dr. Lionel Corbett describes the theories which have been used to explain how belief in God can be invented. According to one theory, our image of God is *nothing but* a result of our childish experience. This theory states that our image of God is said to be similar to a child's use of a teddy bear or blanket. The child uses these items to "carry" the image of the parents when they are unavailable. These items, called transitional objects, make the child feel better or feel comforted, just as the mother makes the child feel better or comforted. When the child is older and more mature, the image of the mother will be more completely integrated, and the child were not need the transitional object any longer to feel secure and comforted. Reductionistic thinkers believe that our image of God is viewed as a special transitional object. Our image of God is *nothing but* an image that makes us feel secure and comforted.

Dr. Corbett points out that although the image of God has the power to help us feel secure and comforted, it does not necessarily follow that God is *nothing but* a transitional object. To conclude that because our image of God is capable of comforting us and therefore God is "only" something created by our minds to comfort us is actually an error in logic. It would be like saying, "I know rice is grown in China, therefore, China is *nothing but* a country where rice is grown."

A second reductionistic view comes out of the work of Alfred Adler. It focuses on the human tendency to want an ideal of perfection. This theory maintains that when mankind's ideal of perfection is made concrete, God is created. Corbett points out that for some people, this theory accurately describes their relationship with God. For them, God does in fact echo their relationship with their parents. To a child, parents are the supreme authority on right and wrong. However, just because some people as adults relate to God in a similar way as they related to their parents as children, it does not necessarily follow that all relationships with God are *nothing but* this. Nor is it necessarily true that God is nothing but a substitute, powerful and perfect parent.

Other reductionists claim that any person who wishes to unite with the Divine is just wishing to enter a regressive experience of union with the mother. Unitive, spiritual experiences are *nothing but* a desire to reenter the womb, to re-experience a time when the child and mother were one. Here again, the theory is simplistic. Although some persons are immature and may be correctly described as regressive, not all persons who are looking for unitive experiences with the Divine are necessarily acting in a regressive mode. They may be highly developed people focused on spiritual issues.

During the years of my early adult life, my spiritual dilemma led me to question whether everything I was taught in my childhood was a lie. I wondered if religion was just my culture's way of teaching a particular type of morality. Was there actually some real reason to believe in a God? My religious dilemma was resolved through a second experience of spiritual revelation.

In the midst of an ordinary day, I suddenly had a deep knowing that God was real. I heard the words "I am real" come to me. It was very much like the experience I had at the time of Ben's death. Standing over his corpse, a message filled my body, stating, "This was supposed to happen this day." I cannot adequately describe these messages. Experiences like this are not ideas that come into one's mind, but are more like a message that fills one's body. It produces a deep sense of knowing that wipes out any doubt. It is the kind of experience you never forget. This kind of experience is not unusual. Dr. Corbett studies modern day religious revelations and finds they are quite common, but most people hesitate to tell others about them.

Spiritual experiences are life changing. The first thing I did was to go back to the church of my childhood. Knowing that on some level the spiritual dimension was real, I reasoned that it was important to return to organized religion. The second thing I did was to relate this embodied spiritual experience to a few close friends. I wanted to share the joy I had of my sense of really knowing God existed. I hoped my experience would be of as much benefit to them as it had been to me.

Although my friends were interested in hearing my story, it could not possibly have the same effect on them as it had on me. They did not have the experience themselves. My telling them about it could not begin to convey its power, nor could telling the story produce the healing effect it had for me. I found myself deeply disappointed. It seemed a pity that something so wonderfully helpful to me could not be helpful to other people as well. After a week, I stopped talking about it to anyone.

I began to attend church regularly, but I found it unfulfilling. The Mass, now in English rather than Latin, seemed ordinary. Although the words of the Mass spoke of spiritual matters, it did not provide the interior, meditative experience of the Latin ritual. Since my present religious revelation was a powerfully rich interior experience, it made me long for more inner spirituality, not a socially-oriented religious life. After a time I became interested in a search for a kind of universal truth by exploring other religious traditions. I hoped to find the basic principles which underlie all spiritual understanding. Ultimately this led me to the same realization found in the work of Joseph Campbell -- all religions are right and true. Religions are to be interpreted symbolically rather than literally.

New Respect for All Religions

Through the years, my ideas about the nature of God continued to evolve. When summarizing my thinking about God and creation before my son's death, I will refer to the God existing "out there" as the Godhead. This Godhead is the original source of everything. Much of the Godhead still exists in its original form, but I think of Creation as something analogous to the "Big Bang Theory." At one point, the point of Creation, the Godhead sent out billions of sparks of "light" that are tiny bits of Itself. These tiny bits of the original Godhead are now all of us. A part of each and every one of us is Divine as well as human. This little part of each of us can not, of course, be compared to the immensity of the Godhead. But it is, nonetheless, a tiny part of the Divine.

It is said that the Hindus recognize they are God. They do not feel they are comparable to the immensity of the original Godhead, or to the Godhead as it currently exists. They realize that within them there exists a "spark" of the Divine. The Hindus acknowledge the Divine within each person they meet by greeting them with hands together and giving a small bow. This small ritual is a statement of their recognition that a spark of the Divine exists in each person they encounter.

This recognition of the divine in each human is more prevalent in the East than the West. Robert Johnson, Episcopal minister and Jungian analyst and author, tells us,

> "There is a perpetual dialogue between East and West. In the West we say that in redemption we worship God and become at peace with Him. We bow our heads to the ground in heavenly Jerusalem and say, "Sanctus, Sanctus, Sanctus" all day long. And the Hindu says you become God in the end. Enlightenment is the moment when you wake up to the fact that it is you who are God." (Johnson, 1986)

Johnson tells a wonderful Hindu story which explores the difference between Enlightenment in the East and Redemption in the West.

The Young Man and the Elephant, a Hindu Tale

A young man came to study with an old master. He made extraordinary development and one day experienced a revelation. He saw that he was God. His teacher checked him out, asked him many questions, and saw that the vision or the realization was true. The young man, even though he was very young, was enlightened. The teacher told the young man so, and the young man was absolutely drunk with joy.

So the young man went away somewhat light in the head and went down a path in the jungle. An elephant with a mahut (its driver) sitting on its head was coming down the other way. The young man, recently enlightened, put his hands on his hips and said, "Get out of my way; I'm God." The mahut tickled the elephants ears and the elephant reached out with a big trunk, picked up the young man (recently enlightened) and plunked him down by the side of the path and went by.

The young man was very put out by this and went back to his teacher and said, `I thought you said I was God' The teacher said, `Yes, indeed you are. But so is the elephant. And so is the mahut' (Johnson, 1986)

Johnson goes on to say, "So however you get at it, if you are a Westerner you come to a state of adoration of God for your salvation. Or if you are an Easterner you become God, but it all amounts to the same thing when you meet the elephant on the path."

I find Johnson's Hindu tale delightful for two reasons. First, its humor is a wonderful way of easing out any grandiosity that could occur from an over identification with the Divine within us. Second, this story allows us to appreciate the Eastern position, while retaining respect for our Western tradition. Both paths take us to the same goal; all religious traditions are good and right. Universal spirituality gives a religious perspective which fits my earliest image of myself as being a spark of the Divine (a spirit) who has come to the earth to live for a time in a body.

Religious traditions struggle with the question of why and how we came to live on earth. Sometimes they address the difficulty a soul has in accepting the challenges of coming to earth to take human form. The Kabbala, part of the Jewish mystical tradition, has a wonderful story about this. It gives an explanation of the process a soul goes through when preparing to leave the spiritual dimension and to take up the difficulties of earthly life.

In the Kabbalistic story, an angel comes to the soul to inform it that it is to come down to earth, come into a body, and be born. The soul protests, saying it does not want to come into the body because it does not wish to leave the radiance of the Godhead. The angel explains to the soul that it has a specific purpose to fulfill. The Kabbalists call it the Teecon. This generally corresponds to Darma in the Hindu tradition, the purpose of a person's life. In the Taoist tradition, it means the mandate of heaven. What is striking is that many religious traditions contain the idea that the soul has to come here for a specific purpose; additionally, the soul is often reluctant to come. When the soul accepts its purpose, it is shown the life it will live and the body it will have. In a treasury of Hebrew wisdom, The Legends of the Jews, a tale is found that goes like this:

The Angel of Forgetfulness, a Jewish Legend

One day the angel takes the soul around, showing it where it will live and where it will die. The soul visits the place it will be buried. Afterwards, the angel places it in its mother's womb. When it is time for it to be born, the same angel again speaks to the soul saying, it is time to enter the open world. The soul protests by asking, "Why do you want me to go out into the world?" The angel answers, "As you were formed against your will, now you will be born against your will. Against your will you will die, and against your will you shall give account of yourself before God, the King of kings." (Ginzberg, 1961) The soul is hesitant to leave the womb, so the angel strikes the baby under its nose, which destroys its memory. (Some say this blow accounts for the indentation we all have between our lip and nose.) The infant forgets all it knew about its past life and its future. Entering the world, it cries because it lost its place of rest and security. (Ginzberg, 1961, p. 58)

The angel, which causes the soul to come into the world with no conscious memory of where it has been or what the purpose of its life is to be, is called The Angel of Forgetfulness.

Corbett says this story has several functions: First, it deals with the difficulty of explaining why anything would leave the realm of the Godhead. Second, it deals with the purposeful nature of all that happens to us. He says, "The parents you have are not an accident. You choose your parents carefully before birth, or your parents are chosen for you. What happens to you is not a coincidence. There is no discrepancy between what you are supposed to be and what was allowed to happen. There is some intention at work.

This story asserts that our coming here has a specific purpose. The parents we are placed with may not be perfect, but they are exactly right for what we are to develop in our lifetime. The suffering we experience is precisely what is necessary for our spiritual growth.

The Angel of Forgetfulness pays another visit to the soul when it becomes time for it to leave life on earth. Once again the soul does not wish to leave. The Legend of the Jews says that when the time comes for the person to die, the angel will appear again. It asks, "Do you remember me?" To which the person replies, "Yes, but why do you come today and not another day?" The angel answers, "To take you away because it is time for your departure." The person weeps and reproaches the angel by saying, "Twice before you have taken me from a place I did not wish to leave, and have brought me into this world." The angel reminds the person, "Did I not tell you that you were formed against your will, and you were born against your will? Against your will you will die, and against your will you will give account of yourself before God." (Ginzberg, 1961, p. 58-59)

This legend was part of my spiritual perspective before the death of my son Ben. After his death I attempted to probe the mystery behind his life and his suffering as it relates to me. If suffering is of potential value, the questions remains: "How can the enormous pain I have gone through since his death bring about my own spiritual growth?" To begin to answer this question, I first applied the wisdom found in that ancient Jewish legend by imagining a dialogue between the angel and my son. It might have gone something like this.

Ben's Angel

"Well, Ben, it is just about time for you to go down there."

"I don't want to go! I want to stay here."

"You have important work to do, and I'll give you a preview of what's in store." With this the angel explained to Ben exactly what the purpose of his life was.

Then the angel explained to Ben, "To fulfill this purpose you will receive three problems: an attention deficit which will make concentration difficult, an anxiety disorder, and a complex depressive condition."

To this Ben shouted, "Oh no you don't! You aren't going to make me go down there and have all of that to deal with!"

"Ben, you have important work to do which can only be done on earth. Now, I'd like you to have a look at the people who will be your parents. The woman down there will be your mother and that man will be your father. They aren't perfect, but they are just what we had in mind for your mission. Here is the body you will have, so if you are ready, I'll just touch you on the nose and here you go." Then on

March 15, 1975, Ben arrived in a state of bewilderment, without the slightest idea of what he was doing here.

From this perspective, Ben's genetically-based depressive condition, his anxiety disorder, and his attention deficit were not meaningless bad luck for him or for me. They were an integral part of what he needed to experience. They were necessary to fulfill the purpose of his life. All the work he did, and all the work I did to help him, were not just a waste of time. They were instead exactly what he would take with him when he left.

Although I was not a perfect mother, I was exactly the mother he needed to fulfill his purpose. Likewise, he was not a perfect son, but he was exactly the right son I needed to fulfill the purpose of my life. The difficulties Ben experienced had caused me great pain, and his death added to my suffering. But his life helped me to grow, and so did his death.

Ben, now in spirit, remembers the explanation the Angel of Forgetfulness gave as the purpose of his life. Someday, I too will remember mine.

Chapter 8

Benefit

A friend who came to see me soon after Ben died said, "This is the worst thing that can happen to a person." At the time I was not sure I agreed with her, but in the many months of grief which followed I came to believe what she said was true.

The Wisdom of Meister Eckhardt

The premise of this book is that suffering can produce personal/spiritual growth. In a sermon entitled, "Blessed are the Poor," thirteenth century Christian scholar, Meister Eckhardt emphasized that the wisdom of God praises poverty of the spirit. It is achieved when one "wills nothing, wants nothing, and knows nothing." The meaning of the phrase "spiritual poverty" confuses many who hear it. Poverty, in modern context, is viewed negatively, as implying a lack of something essential. Eckhardt's use of the term here implies an openness, a receptivity to spiritual growth.

What is meant by spiritual poverty is the same thing that is meant in The Beatitudes, when Jesus says, "Blessed are the poor in spirit, for theirs is the kingdom of heaven." (Matthew 5:3) The concordance for this line in the Bible describes the poor in spirit as persons "of whatever social rank, who recognize their complete dependence on God." Spiritual poverty implies an orientation to God rather than to the things of this earth. In psychological terms, it is an orientation to deep wisdom rather than to the conscious ego; a recognition that ultimately you are not in charge of your life. You are to follow the purpose of your life, the mandate of heaven.

When Eckhardt says, "He alone has true spiritual poverty who wills nothing, wants nothing, and knows nothing," he suggests that if we are to be receptive to a Divine will, we need to have some space for it rather than be completely full of our own ideas. The death of my child may have brought me one step closer to being more open to stop willing, wanting, and knowing. This is what my son's death taught me.

WILLS NOTHING

The word "will" implies the imposing of one's desires onto the world or onto other people. When Ben was alive, I was very much involved with "willing." I was trying everything in my power to help him make his life "work." Along with his father, I made all sorts of attempts to change him, to help him learn how to cope with life here on earth.

When the apostles asked Jesus how they should pray, he responded by giving them the Lord's prayer. The prayer says "...thy kingdom come, thy will be done on earth as it is in heaven." People like myself who are strong willed find the imperative "thy will" rather than "my will" hard to accept.

Stories which point out what happens when we attempt to impose our will instead of aligning ourselves with God's will are helpful to me. John Sanford, Episcopal minister and Jungian analyst, retells in modern day language one of the stories from the Old Testament which illustrates this:

Balaam in the Old Testament

The Hebrews are coming out of the desert into Canaan, into the land of Moab. The King of Moab is afraid that the Hebrews are going to conquer the inhabitants of Moab, just as they conquered other people. So they called on the prophet Balaam to pronounce a curse on the Hebrews. Now, a curse in those days was not just idle words, it really put a hex on you. It had power.

So Balaam, as sort of a free lance prophet, does that sort of thing for hire. He prepares himself, gets on his donkey, and starts off down the road of Moab to pronounce the curse on the Hebrews. Suddenly, the donkey unexpectedly bolts off the path and dashes off. Balaam gets thrown to the ground.

He is furious with his donkey and beats him. He then gets on again, goes a little further, and his donkey does the same thing a second time. This time he is really furious. Again he beats the donkey, goes a little further and it happens again. The donkey unexpectedly dashes off.

By this time Balaam is livid with anger, but then he looks up ahead and sees what the donkey saw all along. He sees the

Malac Yahweh, the dark angel of God, in his path with a drawn sword.

The Angel says, "If you had come one step closer to me I would have killed you. It was your donkey who saved you." The donkey saw the angel all along and turned aside.

Balaam was unable to see the dark, dreadful power. If he had not seen it and did not have the donkey, he would have walked right into the angel; he would have been destroyed because the angel is the dark side of God.

Then Balaam and the angel had a little talk. (The angel did most of the talking.) The angel told Balaam that he could go into Moab and prophesy, but he could prophesy only what Yahweh told him to prophesy. Balaam agreed; he went to Moab and said only those things that Yahweh told him to say. He was allowed to go his way, but now he was going to fulfill the will of Yahweh; and he was not doing his own and the King of Moab's will. (Sanford, 1986)

Sanford then interprets the meaning of this Old Testament story: That is the tale of the dark side of God. If you are going the wrong way and going against the will of God, you aren't going to find the love of God. You are going to find the wrath of God of which the Bible tells us a great deal, what I call the dark side of God. Most of us, when we encounter the dark side of God, think it is the devil. We deem it is evil. It isn't evil. Don't get me wrong: it is very destructive, but what it destroys isn't fit to exist. And if our attitudes aren't fit to exist, it will destroy them, too. That is the dark side of God. And that is why the epistle of the

Hebrews says, "It is a terrible thing to fall into the hands of the living God." (Sanford, 1986)

Contemporary wisdom decrees that we are in charge of our lives, but ancient wisdom gives us a different perspective. In this story from the Old Testament, as in the fairy tale "The Three Feathers" in which the wise King allows fate to determine who will be the new ruler of the kingdom, there is respect for following a will greater than our limited human perspective.

WANTS NOTHING

Wanting means desiring things from the environment and from others. Wanting nothing implies that as the person grows spiritually they will naturally become less demanding, less needy. The person who no longer wants anything is free. Our desires and needs keep us chained, imprisoned in life. The needs and desires for approval make us dependent on others for self-esteem. Similarly, if one's worth is based on financial assets and status associated with one's profession, then in order to maintain self-esteem we may have to stay in a job that might not match our talents, our true destiny. Freeing ourselves from wanting is a major theme in religious stories. Joseph Campbell points out how both Jesus and Buddha dealt with "wanting."

The Three Temptations

Jesus's first temptation was the economic. The Devil remarks that Jesus looks hungry and suggests that he change these stones to bread. Jesus replies, 'Man lives not by bread alone, but by every word out of the mouth of God.' The second temptation was political. The Devil takes Jesus to the top of a mountain where he shows him all the nations in the world. The Devil says, 'You can control all these if you'll bow down to me.' Campbell remarks this is the path taken by some successful politicians. But Jesus refuses this as well. The third temptation was that of spiritual inflation. The Devil begins by flattering Jesus, praising his high spiritual development. He then invites him to go to the top of Herod's Temple and cast himself down. 'God will bear you up, and you won't even be bruised.' But Jesus gives recognition to the fact that he is a man of flesh and blood who should not be allowed to forget the importance of temperance. He replies, 'You shall not tempt the Lord, your God.' Campbell reminds us that these three temptations are just as relevant in today's world as they were in 30 AD.

Buddha also went into the wilderness. After a period of trials, he arrives at the Bo tree of illumination. Here he experiences his three temptations. His are different. They are lust, fear, and submission to public opinion. First, the Lord of Lust shows him his beautiful daughters. These maidens are called Desire, Fulfillment and Regrets-- which signify Future, Present, and Past. The Buddha was not moved because he had detached himself from his sensual character. So Lust turned into the Lord of Death, who flung all the weapons of an army of monsters. But the Buddha found within himself that eternal still point. Again, he was unmoved. The weapons turned into flowers of worship. Then Lust and Death became the Lord of Social Duty. He tried to tempt him into doing what he was told by making him feel ashamed of not being concerned about what was happening in the world. To this the Buddha simply touched the earth with his right hand. Whereupon the voice of the Goddess Mother of the Universe said, 'This my beloved son has already so given of himself to the world that there is no one here to be ordered about. Give up this nonsense,' and his Antagonist dissolved like a dream. The Buddha achieved illumination, spending the next fifty years as teacher.

Campbell goes on to explain how we can be caught by wanting when we find ourselves entangled with desire and fear. He illustrates this by using another story of temptation. Adam and Eve, as parents of our humanity, are caught in a very human dilemma. In the story of the Garden of Eden, Campbell says the symbol of the tree is used "in its temporal aspect, as the tree of knowledge of good and evil, profit and loss, desire and fear. At the right is Eve, who sees the tempter in the form of a child (which means life) offering the apple, and she is moved by desire. Adam, however, from the opposite point of view, sees the serpent-legs of ambiguous temper and is touched with fear. Desire and fear: These are the two emotions by which all life in the world is governed. Desire is the bait; death is the hook. Adam and Eve were moved; the Buddha was not. Eve and Adam brought forth life and were cursed of God; the Buddha taught release from life's fear." (Flowers, 1988, p. 140)

KNOWS NOTHING

Those who 'know nothing' are open to a broader perspective, a wider vision, a greater range of possibilities. They do not focus on preconceived ideas of what might be true. The following ancient story illustrates the importance of not knowing.

The Professor and the Guru

A professor went to the home of an enlightened being for the purpose of gaining spiritual knowledge. The enlightened soul invites him into his house and offers him some tea, which the professor gladly accepts. The host takes out a cup and fills it with tea. He then proceeds to continue pouring the tea into the cup, causing it to overflow. The professor exclaims, "What are you doing? Can't you see that the cup is already full and the tea is falling on the floor?" The enlightened one says, "You are like this tea cup. You are already filled with what you think you know. I cannot teach you because you are incapable of accepting any more."

"Knowing," according to Dr. Corbett, implies thinking and categorizing; sorting things into good, bad, right, and wrong. Campbell says most human beings are caught in this dualistic thinking. Both Corbett and Campbell point out that contrary to the duality found in human thought, the Divine perspective has been depicted in many traditions as unitive. In the divine realm, opposites come together and coexist. If I assume something is "bad" in any absolute sense, then, to quote Corbett, "I make the assumption that I know better than God."

As always, stories illustrate this better than any statements can. This one from the Koran shows how difficult it is for humans to cope with a Divine perspective:

Moses and the Angel, from the Koran

Moses wanted to learn something about the mystery of the Divine perspective. He asked to accompany an angel (the messenger of God) as it goes about the earth doing the will of the Lord. The angel knew that Moses would have great difficulty on the journey. The divine being questioned Moses' ability to tolerate things that are beyond his comprehension. Moses replied by saying, 'If Allah wills, you shall find me patient: I shall not in anything disobey you.'

The angel warned Moses not to ask any questions until he himself spoke to him. Then the two set out. The first thing Moses's companion did was to make a hole in the bottom of the ship. Moses could not stop himself from asking why the angel had done this strange thing. He exclaimed, 'Is it to drown her passengers that you have bored a hole?' 'Did I not tell you,' he replied, 'that you would not bear with me?'

Moses asked for forgiveness by saying 'Do not be angry with me on account of this.'

They continued on their journey and presently met a young man. The angel slew him. Moses exclaimed 'You have killed an innocent man who has done no harm! Surely you have committed a wicked crime.' But the angel again remarked that he did not believe that Moses was capable of remaining silent.

Moses said: 'If ever I question you again, abandon me; for then I should deserve it.'

Finally their travels took them to a city. They found a wall that was on the point of falling over. The angel repaired it. Moses said: 'Had you wished, you could have demanded payment for your labors.' To which the messenger of God replied, 'Now has the time arrived when we must part. But first I will explain to you those acts of mine which you could not bear to watch with patience.'

'Know that the ship belonged to some poor fishermen. I damaged it because in their rear there was a king who was taking every ship by force.' As for the youth, his parents both are true believers, and we feared lest he should plague them with his wickedness and unbelief. It was our wish that their Lord should grant them another in his place, a son more righteous and more filial. As for the wall, it belonged to two orphan boys in the city whose father was an honest man. Beneath it their treasure is buried. Your Lord decreed in His mercy that they should dig out their treasure when they grew to manhood. What I did was not done by my will. 'That is the meaning of what you could not bear to watch with patience.' (Dawood, 1974, pp. 97-98)

John Sanford uses this story from the Koran to make an important point. Even when a person is inclined to be concerned with doing what he thinks is right, he is still limited to a human perspective. There is perhaps another perspective, the Divine perspective, where things look different.

Can Suffering Bring a Gift?

When my son died, a very dear friend said that as painful as this was for me and my family, someday we might be able to see it as a gift. Although it is hard to imagine that the death of our only, very much loved son will someday be seen as a gift, it is helpful to have faith that there is a purpose to his death which we will ultimately see.

What is it about suffering that has the potential of being a gift? Suffering can help us to relinquish a perspective which is too narrow. When things are going well, we tend to be very caught up in willing, wanting, and knowing. When we are successful in imposing our will, when we are getting things we want, when what we think we know is validated by our experiences, there is no motivation to open up to a different perspective. But when things are not working and we are suffering, then we are motivated to be open to another perspective. Dr. Corbett says the Zen position of "no mind" implies giving up the ego position of thinking we know anything for sure. With the relinquishing of knowledge, we let go of categories of what should happen or what must not happen; we open up to the fullness, the wonder, the big picture. Joseph Campbell maintains that all pain originates in the temporality of life, namely, losses. Times of loss are both painful and potentially enriching.

When my father died in 1971, I grieved little. He was 68 years old when he died of a sudden heart attack. As I sat close to his coffin at the visitation, I was struck by a revelation of the essence of his life. My father was an honest man. In the Greek play, Diogenes, the main character carries a lantern and says he is searching the world to find just one honest man. I had the privilege of being raised by such a man. The impact of this insight into the essence of my father's life made me feel proud to be his daughter. It was as if somehow I grew taller and stronger as I sat near his coffin. Suddenly, not only my father's life but, also his death, was a gift.

As I thought about his death and my relationship to him, I suddenly felt an overwhelming need to know more about his relationship with his own father and the circumstances of my grandfather's death. I quickly learned from one of my uncles that my dad had died on exactly the same day, and at exactly the same age as his own father. The meaningful coincidence of those two deaths was a sign to me that there can be something very special, very meaningful, about the day of anyone's death. There are few accidents. Meaning can be found if you follow your inclinations to find it. The unique timing of my father's sudden death increased my respect for the mystery behind our fate.

In the years since my father's death, I continue to feel that both his life and his death are a gift. I do not yet understand how this gift is playing itself out. It continues to be a mystery. The same is true of Ben's death. His life and his death are a gift I will probably never fully understand. It will take years for the mystery to unfold. What is important now is to have an appreciation for his life and for the opportunity to learn spiritual poverty through willing nothing, wanting nothing, and knowing nothing.

Chapter 9

The Mystery of One's Dreams

Dreams, as well as meaningful coincidences, are considered in some traditions to be clues to the Divine will. As children of God, everyone's life is a sacred story. Recognizing the sacredness of every life, some traditions encourage its followers to take their dreams seriously. Much has been written regarding dreams and whether or not they have meaning or relevance in our lives. Jungian' psychology, which emphasizes spirituality, maintains that a person's life is meant to follow a particular course. This plan (the telos, the purpose, the mandate from heaven) is contained within the unconscious. Sometimes we follow our course and sometimes we get lost. Jungians believe dreams arise from the unconscious, and comment on whether or not we are on track. Jungians advocate paying attention to dreams as a resource for sound advice on life. They believe our unconscious contains the total plan for our life: all that has already happened, as well as what lies ahead. Our dreams prepare us for the major events of our lives.

Taking life seriously and taking dreams seriously requires something of us. As in "The Golden Goose," inner life asks that we give something of ourselves to it. The first step in taking dreams seriously begins with remembering them. Since dreams tend to evaporate quickly, these fleeting images can only be retained by telling them to someone else or by writing them down. After they are recorded, the next step is to unlock their symbolism through interpretation.

A simple method of dream interpretation is to write down as many details of the dream as can be recalled. Then, pick out some of the details, write down personal associations with each, and pay attention to the emotions that the dream produces. A one-sentence dream can illustrate how even a simple dream can be interpreted. This dream image consists of a person sitting in a nice restaurant ordering from the menu. The two details picked out by the dreamer were the meal in a nice restaurant, and a menu. The associations the dreamer made to 'meal in a nice restaurant' were: treating herself, a situation in which others serve her, food which nurtures her, and taking care of herself. The associations to 'menu' were: options, choices, decisions, taking only what is exactly right for her, rejecting what is not good for her. The 'feeling tone' of the dream was that the decisions she was making were important, and she needed to think carefully about exactly what was best for her.

Dream interpretation is not a mysterious process. It arises quite naturally from the associations the dreamer makes to the symbols. This seemingly unimportant dream was full of valuable insight. Time spent on interpretation of psychologically important dreams fosters personal growth.

Five Types of Dreams

Not all dreams are equally important, and some distinction can be made between the five different types. Some dreams merely process information gathered during the day. These dreams have very little, if any, psychological significance. There is a theory that our brain has one system for short term memory and slightly different storage for long term memory. It is believed that during sleep the shift from short to long term memory occurs, and the process registers as the images of some of our dreams.

A second type of dream is that which has psychological significance. They comment on how well we are doing at following our fate. Like the one of the dreamer ordering a meal in a restaurant, they are often very simple dreams, but have the potential to give important clues. The symbolism in psychologically significant dreams makes use of memory from our past experiences, is relevant to our present situation, and relates to our future. No one can interpret a dream unless they discover the personal associations each of the symbols has for the dreamer.

The third type of dream is Big Dreams. These occur rarely, and give clues for an entire stage of one's life. We can expect to have one Big Dream for each of the four life stages -- early childhood, youth, mid-life, and old age. Often what distinguishes a Big Dream from other psychologically significant dreams is the power of the dream. When I awaken after having a Big Dream, I am struck by its impact. Unlike other dreams, I am able to remember it for years. To this day I can recall the Big Dream of my childhood. I did not write it down, but it stayed with me nonetheless. When I had my Big Dream in mid-life, I wrote it out immediately upon awakening: I knew it was important, and I did not want to forget any of the details. I then sat down and typed it out. The recording of this dream got much more care and attention than I usually give dreams. I tried to figure out its meaning, but I also realized it would be five to ten years before I could begin to really understand what it meant. Even then there would be elements of it that I would never fully comprehend. These Big Dreams comment on the theme or task of a decade or two.

The fourth type are precognitive dreams, which serve to prepare one for upcoming events. Precognitive dreams also tend to be powerful. They get our attention. Whether or not a dream is precognitive is not easy to discern. Even when it is correctly recognized as precognitive, the exact interpretation of the dream is not always literally true. For example, many women near mid-life dream they give birth to a new baby. Usually these women do not become pregnant in the literal sense. The dreams often mean something new and creative which comes from within themselves is about to enter into their lives. Similarly, a dream of a death of someone else may not mean the literal death of that person. Instead, it may signify a loss of some aspect of their own life. The person who "dies" in the dream is symbolic of a part of their own self that needs to go. The unconscious chooses the death of another person because he or she is the best representative of a characteristic they need to discard or release within themselves.

All of us have heard stories of precognitive dreams that literally come true. Someone will dream of the death of a friend or relative only to find out in a day or two that it actually happened. Sometimes we question the accuracy of these tales, but if it ever happens in your own family, you will probably take it seriously. This is what occurred to my mother preceding the death of one of my sisters.

My mother's precognitive dream took the form of a waking dream rather than a nighttime dream. I use the term "waking dream" because some psychologists hypothesize that the unconscious is producing dream images all the time, but we do not perceive them in the daytime when we are active. We usually experience dreams only at night, when outside stimulation is shut down and the quieter, inner activity can be heard. It is analogous to the fact that we only see stars at night. The stars are there all the time, but during the day we can not see them because the sun is so bright. It is only in the darkness, after the sun sets, that we are able to see the stars. So it is with the images arising from the unconscious. During the daytime we are active. Stimuli are constantly coming into our eyes and ears, and interfere with our ability to see the images from the unconscious. Another analogy is the music that is piped into offices and elevators. It is playing softly in the background all the time, but it is only audible when everyone is quiet.

My mother's waking dream came to her during a time when she was sitting very still. My parents were dairy farmers and my mother was usually very busy. She had a large family, common at the time, consisting of seven daughters and two sons. Her second daughter, Ellen, had a heart condition probably caused by the rheumatic fever she had as a young child. The doctor told my parents Ellen was not to overexert herself. Ellen did housework but was not allowed to work in the fields or in the barn like the rest of us. This also meant she could not play the energetic games we all loved to play. We lived with one strict rule: "Ellen can't run." You can imagine how she felt standing by, watching the rest of us enjoying ourselves.

Ellen attended our hometown's two room school house. The Ellen-Can't-Run Rule, enforced at home by our watchful parents, was also carefully enforced for many years at school by our oldest sister, Shirley. When the day came that Shirley graduated from eighth grade and moved on to high school, Ellen saw her chance and made a secret announcement not meant for grown-up ears. Now that she was in the eighth grade and the oldest in school, there was no one to stop her from doing what she wanted. She intended to run with the other children, playing the games forbidden to her for so many years.

It was about this time that my mother began to have a waking dream. It came to her during the day when she was forced to sit very still, when she did the milking. The milking was done by machine, but in order to make the milk machine work more efficiently and quickly, my parents would sit very quietly by the cow and apply some pressure on the apparatus. I have done this type of work myself and it produces a contemplative state of mind. It is similar to how you feel when you are driving along a quiet freeway in the country with nothing but the markings on the road to look at. You are alert while driving, but are also lulled into a kind of trance. It was in this alert but quiet state my mother had her waking dream image.

The dream image consisted of seeing a female figure in a coffin. My mother could clearly see the white dress the dead figure wore, but she could not tell who the person was. Although my mother did not have any idea who this female figure was, the image made her feel extremely sad, and she found herself crying. My mother knew my sister had a heart condition, but she did not realize it could be fatal. Our family doctor had only indicated to her that Ellen was not to run or do any strenuous work. He had not said Ellen might die if she overstrained her heart. My parents always felt the doctor acted properly; his recommendations were strictly followed, but our family was not overly burdened with continuous fears for Ellen's well being.

My mother did not have the slightest idea to whom the dream images referred. Dreams produce images arising from the depths of our unconscious that usually are not understood on the level of our conscious (rational thinking) mind. Dream images also bring forth strong emotion. My mother experienced grief with her recurring waking dream.

On September 13, 1948, my sister was playing during the lunch recess at school. Feeling pain in her chest, she ran from the playground towards the front of the church where she fell and died. When planning for the funeral, my mother remembered the dream image of the female figure in a white dress; she made the connection and understood its meaning. My parents tried to find a white dress in which to bury my sister. Because it was autumn it was impossible to find a white dress in the stores, they purchased a white blouse to dress her for the burial.

I, too, had a precognitive dream before my son's death. My dream image produced fear. It is my belief that precognitive dreams serve to prepare us for major events without interfering with them. It seems as if dream images give us enough information to prepare us for the painful events of our life without giving us so much information that the future interferes with the present.

When looking at precognitive dreams, we learn that some of them are to be interpreted on a symbolic level, while others are literally true. When I had my precognitive dream before Ben's death, it was that I had breast cancer and was going to die. The feeling tone of the dream was great fear. One can never be absolutely sure to what these dreams refer. I do not know any sure way to tell the difference. What I did was to trust my intuition. The interpretation I gave the dream was -- fear of death. Like my mother, I did not have the slightest idea it would turn out to be the death of one of my children.

The fifth type of dream is similar to the near-death experience. In an actual Near Death Experience (NDE), the person comes close to death and experiences being out of their body. The person often sees the spirit of friends and relatives who have died come to meet them and help them with the transition. Later, a loving, warm spirit described as "a being of light" will appear before them.

Jung's Near Death Experience

In his autobiography, Memories, Dreams and Reflections, Carl Jung recalls his own Near Death Experience. Early in 1944 he broke his foot, and this accident produced a heart attack. Jung wrote that when unconscious he experienced "deliriums and visions which must have begun when I hung on the edge of death and was being given oxygen and camphor injections." (Jaffe, 1963) The images were so powerful he thought he must surely be near death. The nurse told him later that he seemed to have a bright glow around him, a phenomenon she often saw when caring for dying patients. Jung did not know whether he was dreaming or in some sort of ecstatic state, but he felt he was up in space. The earth below him was "bathed in a gloriously blue light." He saw the blue sea and the outline of some of the continents. He did not see the whole earth. He was above India and Ceylon, and the earth had a silvery gleam through its marvelous blue light. As Jung floated in space he became aware of a black meteorite, the size of a big house, close to him. Within the huge dark stone was a small antechamber.

There were steps at the entrance of the chamber. As Jung approached, more strange things began to happen. Everything was taken away from him. All of his earthly goals, all he wished for, everything he thought was removed from him. (This part of Jung's story is reminiscent of Eckhardt's "He alone has true spiritual poverty who wills nothing, wants nothing, knows nothing." Jung's NDE lent credence to those insights into profound spiritual experience.)

Jung described the stripping away process as being painful. What was left with was the experiences he had during his lifetime: all he had done and all that had happened around him. What he had left was his life history. The stripping away left him with "a feeling of extreme poverty, but at the same time of great fullness." (Is it an accident that Eckhardt used the term "spiritual poverty?") Jung no longer wanted or desired anything. When it first happened, Jung recalled feeling pillaged, annihilated. But then, quite quickly, being stripped of everything came to be of no consequence. The pull of earthly concerns were all in the past. He felt no regret or loss at what had been taken away. He wrote, "On the contrary: I had everything that I was, and that was everything."

As he approached the antechamber, something filled his mind. He realized he was going to meet all the people he had a connection with throughout eternity. There he would finally know the historical pattern of his life. Jung wrote,

> "My life as I lived it had often seemed to me like a story that had no beginning and no end. I had the feeling that I was a historical fragment, an excerpt for which the preceding and succeeding text was missing. My life seemed to have been snipped out of a long chain of events, and many questions had remained unanswered. Why had it taken this course? Why had I brought these particular assumptions with me? What use had I made of them? What will follow? I felt sure that I would receive an answer to all these questions as soon as I entered the rock temple. There I would learn why everything had been thus and not otherwise. There I would meet the

> people who knew the answer to my question about what had been before and what would come after." (Jaffe, 1963)

While thinking about this, an image floated up. It was the image of the physician who was treating Jung for his heart attack. As they stood face to face, a mute communication took place between them. Without words, the physician let Jung know he must return to earth. It was not yet time for him to die. The moment he received the message, the vision stopped, and Jung's consciousness was once again back in the hospital bed.

Profoundly disappointed, he felt that all he had gone through was useless. The pain of being stripped of earthly concerns was endured for nothing. Jung was deprived of entering the antechamber in the meteorite temple, of becoming reunited with the people he belonged to in the spiritual realm. In his disappointment, he came to look upon earthly life as artificial, a place where each of us is living life isolated from each other. Now he would have to go back and try to pretend this solitary life was important. Life in the world seemed like a prison to him. Jung had been glad to leave earth and now he would have to return. Jung was resentful towards his doctor, for it was he who had brought him back to life, yet Jung was also concerned about him. Intuitively he realized the physician's own life was in danger. Appearing to him as he had implied that his entrance into the spiritual domain was near. Jung's intuitions told him his physician was about to die instead of him. He tried to talk about it, but the physician appeared not to understand. Being irritated at having to live, angry at his physician for bringing him back to life, and frustrated at not being understood, Jung became a thoroughly incorrigible patient.

In fact, Jung was the last patient the doctor ever treated. The physician became ill soon afterwards and died.

Dreams Before Dying

Marie Louis von Franz has done extensive work on the dreams of persons who were dying. In her book, On Dreams and Death, she writes that the dreams of some people who are close to death are similar to NDE's. She compared the dream motifs of people close to death with the descriptions of momentary "near-death experiences," as described in literature. She writes that although the subject matter in the dreams

> "do not differ essentially from the imagery of the death experience, the dreams are far more subtle and richer in imagery. Compared to dreams, near-death experiences appear schematic and more specifically culture-formed. The dreams are in themselves more graphic and detailed. The analysis of older people provides a wealth of dream symbols that psychically prepare the dreamers for impending death." (von Franz, 1987a)

Von Franz gave an example of a dream of an older man who was dying of a lung disease. In the dream, he left the hospital and walked toward the edge of the city. Here he met the image of a wise man who told him he must decide if he was to continue living and doing his earthly work, or if he wanted to leave his body. The dreamer came to understand that his sickbed was his work. Two days later the man died. Von Franz (1987a, p. 76) interpreted the dream to mean "that it is important to meet death consciously, that one should make up one's mind about it, so to speak." That the sickbed was identical to the man's work indicates the dreamer was now to focus his energy and efforts on his dying.

In the dream of the dying person, a dead relative or someone who is recently deceased often appears. Von Franz says so many incidents of this phenomenon have been recorded that some people have come to believe that "the dead come to fetch the dying and assist them in their adjustment to the after-death condition." (von Franz, 1987a, p.77)

On a personal level, my mother-in-law had a precognitive dream as part of her death process. Our son died on May 31, 1989. At the end of November of the same year, my husband's father came to us with the news that Garry's mother had cancer. Her illness initially produced little emotional impact on us because we were already grieving. Our main concern for her was that she receive care which was sensitive to her needs and wishes. We wanted her to be as comfortable as possible during her illness.

On December 6, her surgery revealed cancer of the pancreas. The doctors told us she had four to six months to live. For six weeks after her surgery, she was able to leave her house to visit with friends. Afterwards she was house-bound. Because I worked full time, Saturday mornings was my time to spend with her. I wanted to be helpful to her in the dying process.

Elisabeth Kubler-Ross wrote in her book, Death, The Final Growth Stage, of the enormous amount of psychological and spiritual growth that can happen in a relatively short time. It is helpful for the dying person to be viewed as an individual for whom the physical body is being reduced (in preparation for its being discarded) while the psyche/spirit is expanding. This transformation of emphasis away from the physical body to the spirit may not always be obvious. There is a tendency to over-emphasize the physical body during illness because it obviously needs care. Those who choose to pay attention to the psychological growth of the dying person see that in some, the personality blossoms. This was the case with my mother-in-law.

As the weeks went by she became weaker, but we were able to have many quiet conversations, often interrupted by her intermittent naps. When she awoke one day we talked about how easily she fell asleep. Remembering the work of von Franz, I asked her if she had any dreams. Her answer was, "I never dream." The way she answered the question gave me the impression she not only did not remember any dreams, but did not think her dreams would be important. I wondered if she would someday have a dream in which her mother or one of her deceased siblings would welcome her into the next world.

During the last ten days of her life my mother-in-law entered the hospital. An extra bed was put into her room so Garry's dad could be with her during the night. One morning she awoke around four a.m. When her husband's eyes opened shortly afterwards, she motioned for him to come to her bed.

She said she had seen Ben, her sister, and her mother. Ben and her sister were standing together looking at her. Her sister was waving her forward as if to tell her to come. Ben was not moving but was looking at her intently, with a great big smile on his face. Her mother was close to them, sitting in a chair. This dream was especially helpful to her. Earlier in her illness she had been afraid to die and resisted even talking about her illness being fatal. After the dream she was more accepting and less fearful of the process. The dream prepared her for the transition.

What is the purpose of dreams? Dreams, like meaningful coincidences, give clues to the course our life is meant to take. When they are interpreted symbolically, they tell us if we are following the path intended for us to follow. Dreams also prepare us to accept the painful changes our conscious mind rebels against. If we are willing to pay attention to the clues our unconscious provides, and to respect the inevitability of these changes, we can be spared some of the unnecessary suffering that occurs when we insist our tragedies should not have happened.

Chapter 10

The Surprising Side of Tragedy

After Ben's death, my husband and I began attending a support group for those whose loved ones died from suicide. In the first few months, as the newest victims, we shared the story of our recent tragedy and were grateful for the presence of others who knew what we were going through. As the months went by, other newcomers joined our ranks when suicide touched their lives.

In the many books written about suicide survivors, authors say we tend to experience guilt and shame. Some survivors do feel this, but I did not, and some survivors I meet claim they did not either. Guilt and shame are unnecessary suffering that can be decreased by giving the survivor accurate information about the nature of conditions such as depression and anxiety disorders. When survivors come to understand the seriousness of the condition that caused the death, they come to see there is no more reason for them to feel guilty or ashamed than if the deceased had died of a heart attack or cancer.

For a time, most survivors will likely go through a stage of feeling "if only I would have done this or that the suicide could have been prevented." Many survivors also feel they somehow **should** have known more about the pain their love one felt and **should** have tried more to help him or her. I take the position that **everyone does the best they can**. No one is responsible for another person's fate.

Suicide survivors are much more like anyone else who loses someone suddenly than they are different. For a few months, my husband and I attended a second grief support group. It was for parents who lost an older child for any reason. The pain of losing our child suddenly through suicide did not seem different from the pain other parents had from losing their child unexpectedly through an accident or short illness. Either way, we felt unprepared for the loss. Our grief was like that of the other parents. It was characterized by sadness, anger, and disappointment.

SADNESS

The origin of the word *grief* means to be cheated. Losing a child makes you feel cheated: cheated of their future and cheated of your own. My words are feeble attempts to describe the sadness at being deprived the company of someone you loved so much and who loved you in return.

ANGER

I do not know how many times I slammed car doors in the years since Ben died, but my poor car really took a beating. Being angry at the person who died (something many people feel) or just generally angry that it had to happen at all (the source of my feelings) is a necessary and important emotion to express. Luckily, the car door could accept my anger, and I could express it without doing much damage to myself or it.

DISAPPOINTMENT

After coming to a measure of acceptance, one is often left with a sense of disappointment. My husband lost his son, his hunting companion, his fishing buddy, and the person who accompanied him on his daily walks. Prone to depression himself, our son's death was almost more than he could bear.

Our daughter lost her only sibling. When I was pregnant, she wanted a baby sister. She got over her disappointment by realizing that he was still a baby, and all babies can be a joy. As this brother grew up, though, he was more of a nuisance than most younger brothers. His attention deficit meant he lacked the social skills it took to play with other children; he was impulsive, and could not concentrate or follow the rules of their games.

His depression and anxiety made him overly sensitive, fearful, irritable, and easily angered. In most activities he was more disruptive than fun to have around. My daughter wanted me to have more children, but because of the genetic nature of Ben's condition, I was hesitant. Life has been disappointing for my daughter. Her family did not turn out as she would have liked.

Grief produces self pity, and for a time this pity is extremely necessary. No one should be rushed through the grief process even by those who genuinely want them to feel better. But during the pain, it is good to know that loss is not just a meaningless accident, not just bad luck. There is something to be gained from our suffering.

FINDING A PERSONAL MEANING

What has Ben's life and death given to me? It taught or reaffirmed these beliefs:

1. *Those who suffer can have an everlasting, eternal reward which serves to balance the pain they experience. They can use their suffering for spiritual purposes by trusting in the meaning of their lives.*

2. *There is a time for everything; a time to laugh and a time to cry. When we trust fate to take us in the right direction, even when it is painful, we will fulfill all the tasks we were meant to have. Our life can have wholeness; it can be balanced.*

3. *Our current suffering is a preparation for some future purpose we may not yet see.*

4. *A time of suffering can reorient one to what is really important. As Frankl suggests, when someone is irrevocably lost, we have the opportunity to look deep within ourselves to find what is meaningful to us.*

5. *To discover personal meaning, coincidences and dreams offer clues to the mystery of life.*

I am fond of this saying: "Nothing is anything, it is just an opportunity for something." My loss is not only tragic, it is an opportunity for growth. I could ask, "Why did Ben die?" I can also ask, "Why was I born?" If life has a purpose, the best clues to this purpose lie in what we take with us when we leave: our experiences and the growth they produce. Suffering and loneliness are my greatest opportunities for personal/ spiritual growth.

When Ben died, a good friend predicted we would ultimately realize the gift his life and his death were to us. As I struggle to will nothing, want nothing, and know nothing, I come to see that although my father's death was a gift to me, Ben's was even more. Each of their lives was unique, and each of their deaths gave me something different.

Judged by outward standards of success, part of Ben's life was a failure. He was not successful at school, was not good at team sports, and was not the most popular youngster among his peers. Judged by the real purpose of his life (to grow spiritually and provide others the opportunity to grow) his life was a success. The Angel of Forgetfulness sent him to earth without any memory of the purpose of his life. Now Ben remembers. I will always be grateful to him for the years he spent with us.

Works Cited

Bolen, J.S., MD (1984). Goddesses in Everywoman. New York: Harper Row.

Campbell, J. (1990). Transformations of myth through time. New York: Harper & Row.

Dawood, D.A. (Ed.). (1974). The Koran. London: Penguin Books.

Flowers, B.S. (Ed.). (1988). Joseph Campbell: The power of myth, with Bill Moyers. New York: Doubleday.

Frankl, V.E. (1959). Man's search for meaning. New York: Washington Square Press.

Fuller, Buckminster. (1981). Critical Path. New York: St Martin Press

Ginzberg, L. (1961). The legends of the Jews. Philadelphia: the Jewish Publication Society of America.

Hoberman, H.M., Ph.D. (1989). Completed suicide in children and adolescents: A review. In B.D. Garfinkel (Ed.), Adolescent suicide: Recognition, treatment, and prevention. New York: Haworth.

Jaffe', A. (Ed.). (1963). Memories, Dreams, Reflections by C. G. Jung. New York: Vintage Books.

Johnson, R. (1986). Interior Feminine in Relationships (Audio Tape), Human Relations Institute

Manheim, R. (Ed.). (1977). Grimm's tales for young and old. New York: Anchor Press/Doubleday.

May, R. (1975). The courage to create. New York: Bantam Books.

McKay, M. & Fanning, P. (1987). Self esteem. Oakland, California: New Harbinger Publications.

von Franz, M. (1970). Interpretation of fairytales. Dallas, Texas: Spring Publications, Inc.

von Franz, M. (1987a). On dreams and death. Boston: Shambhala.

von Franz, M. (1987b). Shadow and evil in fairytales. Dallas, Texas: Spring Publications, Inc.

Wallis, C., & Willwerth, J. (1992, July 6). Schizophrenia: A new drug brings patients back to life. Time, pp. 53-55

Weissman, M., Ph.D. (1991). Panic and suicidal behavior. Lifesavers: The Newsletter of the American Suicide Foundation.

Wrobleski, A. & McIntosh. (1988). Problems of suicide survivors. In E. Chigier (Ed.), Grief and bereavement in contemporary society: Volume one: Psychodynamics. London: Freund Publishing House Ltd.

Wrobleski, A. (1991). Suicide survivors: A guide for those left behind. Minneapolis, Minnesota

Further References

Burns, D.D., MD (1980). Feeling good: The new mood therapy. New York: The New American Library, Inc.

Fieve, F.R., MD (1975). Moodswings. New York: Bantam Books.

Gawain, S. (1978). Creative Visualizations. New York: Bantam Books.

Gold, M.S. (1987). The good news about depression. New York: Bantam Books.

Harris, G. Gods & Pharaohs from Egyptian mythology. New York: Schocken Books.

Klerman, G., Weissman, M., Rounsaville, B., & Chevron, E. (1984). Interpersonal psychotherapy of depression. New York: Basic Books, Inc.

Kubler-Ross, Elisabeth. (1975). Death, the final growth stage. New Jersey: Prentice-Hall, Inc.

Larson, D.E., MD (Ed.). (1990). Mayo Clinic family health book. New York: William Morrow and Company, Inc.

McKnew, D.H., Cytryn, L., & Yahraes, H. (1983). Why isn't Johnny crying? Coping with depression in children. New York: Norton & Company.

Papolos, D., and Papolos, J. (1992). Overcoming depression. New York: Harper Perennial.

Sargent, M. (1989). Depressive illnesses: Treatment brings new hope. U.S. Department of Health and Human Services. National Institute of Mental Health.

Sargent, M. (1990). Helping the depressed person get treatment. US Department of Health and Human Services. National Institute of Mental Health.

Sarnoff Schiff, H. (1977). The bereaved parent. New York: Penguin Books

Sheehan, D.V. (1983). The anxiety disease. New York: Bantam Books.

Wrobleski, A. (1991). Suicide survivors: A guide for those left behind. Minneapolis, Minnesota

Veninga, R.L. (1985). A gift of hope: How we survive our tragedies. New York: Ballantine Books.

Index

—E—

—F—

—G—

—W—

—Y—

—Z—

About the Author

Trudy Carlson never intended to write this book. Ben's death made her put aside her other writing in order to write the story of his life. She wanted to record everything about the problems she observed during the various stages of his life; all the things she did to help him, and her attempts to obtain treatment for his condition.

As she worked she discovered she had four separate topics. The first became the book, The Suicide of My Son: A Story of Childhood Depression. This is now also published as two separate works: Ben's Story and Depression in the Young.

Learning Disabilities: How to Recognize & Manage Learning & Behavioral Problems in Children contrasts Ben's ADD (Attention Deficit Disorder) with her own personal struggle with dyslexia. She explains why she was able to manage her problems and why Ben's were overwhelming.

Tragedy: Finding a Hidden Meaning: How to Transform the Tragedies in Your Life into Personal Growth, explores the personal and spiritual growth that can emerge from loss. "Meaning makes most things endurable, perhaps everything."

Suicide Survivors Handbook: A Guide for the Bereaved and Those Who Wish to Help Them, deals with the major issues confronting the survivor. It also gives a wealth of practical advice on what is most helpful during recovery from grief.

ORDER FORM

Telephone orders: Call Toll Free: **1-800-296-7163**
Please have your Visa or MasterCard number ready
For mail orders make checks payable to:: **Benline Press, 118 N. 60th Ave E., Duluth, MN. 55804.**

Please send the following books. I understand that I may return any books for a full refund -- for any reason, no questions asked.

Suicide Survivors' Handbook: A Guide to the Bereaved and Those Who Wish to Help Them $14.95 ________

The Suicide of My Son: A Story of Childhood Depression
$16.95 ________

Tragedy: Finding a Hidden Meaning -- How to Transform the Tragedies in Your Life into Personal Growth
$14.95 ________

Learning Disabilities: How to Recognize and Manage, Learning and Behavioral Problems in Children
$14.95 ________

Sales Tax: Add 6.5% for books shipped to Minnesota ________

Shipping: Book Rate: $2.00 for the first book and 75 cents for each additional book. (Surface shipping may take three to four weeks) Airmail: $3.50 per book
Total ________

Payment: __ check __ credit card
Card Number:____
Name on card:____
Exp. Date _____/_____